William C. (William Carey) Richards

**The Apostle of Burma**

A Missionary Epic in Commemoration of the Centennial of the Birth of Adoniram

Judson

William C. (William Carey) Richards

**The Apostle of Burma**
*A Missionary Epic in Commemoration of the Centennial of the Birth of Adoniram Judson*

ISBN/EAN: 9783337093143

Printed in Europe, USA, Canada, Australia, Japan

Cover: Foto ©Thomas Meinert / pixelio.de

More available books at **www.hansebooks.com**

# THE APOSTLE OF BURMA

## *A MISSIONARY EPIC*

IN COMMEMORATION OF THE CENTENNIAL OF THE BIRTH OF

## ADONIRAM JUDSON

BY

WILLIAM C. RICHARDS

BIRTHPLACE OF DR. JUDSON, MALDEN, MASS.

BOSTON 1889
LEE AND SHEPARD Publishers
NEW YORK C. T. DILLINGHAM

## TO

## EDWARD JUDSON, D.D.

———◆———

DEAR friend, to thee, thy noble father's son,
May I, with fitness unimpeachable,
These humble lays inscribe, which seek to tell
What he in Gautama's great realm had done,
What sought to do, what suffered, and what won
Of guerdons, such as dauntless Paul befell,
Seeking in lesser Asia to dispel
Like heathen glooms thy great sire gazed upon.

Apostles of the Gentiles both, their names
At the far ends of nineteen centuries ring;
And thine with Timothy's I'm fain to match,
Since thou hadst grace (as he from Paul) to catch
His zeal and spirit, of whose worth I bring
These echoes of the Christian world's acclaims.

# PREFACE.

A POEM should not need a preface, albeit its occasion may demand it. It is quite probable that the *raison d'être* of this book is to be found less in itself than in what has occasioned its production and publication; to that, therefore, the author may properly refer these advance words. Of all centennial periods which have challenged public attention of late, there has been none of higher, and hardly of broader, interest than the hundredth anniversary of the birth of the man who in the heart of one vast continent has inaugurated and prosecuted with wonderful energy, and equally wonderful success, a work which has stirred the heart of another continent with an enthusiasm of interest and a fervor of participation scarcely paralleled in the annals of Christian philanthropy.

A score of biographies, and multitudinous sketches in magazines and journals, have made the name of JUDSON a household word throughout the length and breadth of Christendom. Its utterance kindles yet a light in the eye and a glow in the bosom of millions of sympathetic men and women, old and young, who know, in part at least, what he, and noble women sharing his name, did — and endured in doing — to convert the great empire of Burma from idolatry and superstition to divine worship and intelligent faith in God. It is the centenary of his birthday that this poem commemorates. This is the occasion of its being, and of its being made a part of the cordial celebration of it. It was in the heart of its author to lay a laurel wreath, not upon his grave, for that was hollowed in the depths of the Indian Ocean, but upon his enshrinement in the memory and devotion of all hearts that throb to-day with gratitude to him for his noble self-sacrifice, and more to God, who inspired him with his seraphic zeal, and crowned his toils and tortures with trophies, the number and value of which will not be fully known until the books of Time's completed annals are opened in Eternity.

To link his achievements, his aspirations, his tribulations, and his triumphs with epic verse, if yet a daring design, has been attempted with an oppressive sense of inadequacy for its best performance; and hence the poet ingenuously casts his work behind the great occasion of its doing, and seeks rather the Divine approval of its purpose than human applause for its measures or manner.

CHICAGO, Oct. 1, 1888.

# CONTENTS.

|  | PAGE |
|---|---|
| INVOCATION | xv |
| THE THEME | 1 |
| CHRISTIAN LETHARGY | 3 |
| WILLIAM CAREY | 4 |
| THE TWINNED HEROES | 5 |
| JUDSON'S CHANGE OF VIEWS | 6 |
| ITS RESULTS | 8 |
| THE EAST INDIA COMPANY | 9 |
| BUDDHISM | 10 |
| AT RANGOON | 12 |
| A DEFEATED VOYAGE | 13 |
| A TRYING ABSENCE | 15 |
| A CHRISTIAN ZAYAT | 17 |
| FIRST BURMAN BAPTISM | 18 |
| QUIET TOILS | 19 |
| GATHERING CLOUDS | 20 |
| DEATH AT THE THRONE | 21 |
| JUDSON AT COURT | 22 |

## CONTENTS.

|   |   |
|---|---|
| Encouragement | 23 |
| Mrs. Judson in America | 25 |
| Her Return with Help | 26 |
| A Home in Ava | 27 |
| A Royal Pageant | 28 |
| Mrs. Judson's Heroism | 30 |
| Ava's Death-Prison | 31 |
| Oung-Pen-La | 35 |
| Songs of Sorrow | 35 |
| Retribution | 42 |
| Deliverance | 43 |
| Maloun | 44 |
| Ava's Redemption-Fee | 45 |
| Death Defeated | 46 |
| Capture of Pugan | 48 |
| Terror at Ava | 49 |
| Freedom | 50 |
| The British Camp | 51 |
| A Little Comedy | 52 |
| Honors of War | 53 |
| Return to Rangoon | 55 |
| Another Promised Land | 56 |
| His Conscientiousness | 57 |
| Death of Mrs. Judson | 58 |
| New Home at Maulmain | 60 |
| A Mystic Passion | 62 |
| Jungle Solitude | 63 |
| The Awakening | 65 |

## CONTENTS.

| | PAGE |
|---|---|
| THE KARENS | 66 |
| KO-THAH-BYU | 66 |
| JUNGLE TOURS | 67 |
| A MARRIAGE-SONG | 68 |
| OLD PROME | 70 |
| RETREAT | 73 |
| RETROSPECTS | 76 |
| SHADOWS | 78 |
| THE BURMAN BIBLE | 80 |
| THE ISLE OF FRANCE | 81 |
| A BURMESE LEXICON | 83 |
| THE SHADOW OF DEATH | 84 |
| HEROIC PURPOSE FRUSTRATED | 86 |
| A GRAVE AT ST. HELENA | 87 |
| DR. JUDSON IN AMERICA | 88 |
| A ROMANTIC MARRIAGE | 90 |
| RETURN TO BURMA | 91 |
| RANGOON TRIALS | 94 |
| AGAIN AT MAULMAIN | 96 |
| THE SHINING MARK | 98 |
| HIS LAST VOYAGE | 99 |
| DEATH AND BURIAL AT SEA | 100 |
| HIS WORK | 101 |
| APOSTROPHIC | 102 |
| NOTES | 105 |

# THE APOSTLE OF BURMA

## INVOCATION.

ETERNAL Son of God, for Thy high worth,
    In my unworthiness, I cry to Thee,
  My help, my breath, my soul's resource to be,
And send from heaven to this Thy native earth,

A spark of that song-fire which filled the sky,
    Above the wondering Bethlehem shepherds' fold,
    With angel raptures for its joy foretold, —
Thine own incomparable birth-melody.

In that divine evangel was begun
    Heaven's open mission to our ruined race;
    Chief Herald, Thou, of that redeeming grace,
Through Earth's remotest cycles thence to run.

O first Apostle of God's love to men,
    Whose birth through rolling centuries we sing,
    Grant me with strength, 'neath my faint trembling,
Strains of Judea's song to wake again.

## INVOCATION.

One century back my harp is fain to bring,
   Its feeble strings in Thy strength only strong,
   With deep intent to frame a fitting song
Of one, the servant of Thyself, his King:

Who bore Thy gospel to the distant East,
   Beyond the shining of Thy natal star;
   Of heralds of Thy Cross to lands afar,
To us the greatest, to himself the least.

Not Burma's sons his errand to receive
   Than were Thy kindred Thee to love more loath;
   The spell of sin hung darkly over both,
Gentile and Jew, alike, slow to believe.

As Thou wast light to him from heathen skies,
   And from his crosses raised him to his crown,
   Thy glory shines for us in his renown,
And to Thy glory may this song arise.

# THE APOSTLE OF BURMA.

SING with grief, my lays are less than fit
   The greatness of my theme to magnify;
   With gladness more, my theme is yet so high,
My little skill shall scarce disparage it.

That theme — the life, the toils, the triumphs too,
   Of Burma's first Apostle of the Cross,
   Our century's honor, and no less its loss —
Looked with the eye of sacred seer through.

I sing of JUDSON [1] — from his ardent youth,
   With a strong zeal for Christian service fired,
   With Christly passion for the work inspired,
To lighten heathen gloom with heavenly truth.

With gifts to envy, both of form and mind,
  With visions fair and bright life's vistas down,
  He chose a cross, for whom a civic crown
Or cleric chaplet Time was sure to find.

To life-long exile from his native land,
  In perils and privations vague yet sure,
  The charm that lured his feet had need been pure,
Beyond a sordid sense to understand.

Nor went he forth with little reck of life,
  Alone, adventurous, and prodigal;
  From fact or fable whence shall we recall
The faultless type of that heroic wife —

Whose sweetness and whose strength, with equal power,
  Upbore his spirit and inspired his soul,
  What waves soe'er of woe might o'er him roll;
And with love's sunshine flushed his darkest hour.

On her lone grave, beneath the Hopia tree,[2]
  From tender eyes which never saw her face,
  Rain tears of love, and heavy with grief's grace,
That her sweet sainted life so brief should be.

Ah, woman's love, in cottage, camp, and cell,
  Has dauntless smiled at want and pain and chains;
  But its transcendent record yet remains
For mission-annals of the Cross to tell.

WHEN in his youthful breast the sacred fire
    Of mission zeal to holy flame upsprung,
    Thick mists of lethargy the Church o'erhung,
That well might check and chill his strong desire.

The great commission of the risen Christ,
    That gave all nations of the world at large,
    For holy teaching, to His followers' charge,
When on the Mount they met in farewell tryst,

Was half forgot, or, if remembered still,
    Had lost the subtile spell with which it stirred
    The first disciples of the heavenly Word,
In face of foes, His mandate to fulfil.

The triumphs of the Cross in martyr days,
    The modern Church extolled in lofty strain,
    But doubted if, to win the world again,
The warfare need be waged in martyr ways.

For that great end the power was God's alone,
    And none might help, as none could stay, His hand:
    In His own time the Cross, in every land,
For His own name and glory, should have sway.

Oh, fatal spell on Christian souls to fall
    Of unbelief, that checks the tides of grace,
    Whose flow and force, alone, shall save the race,
And make the Christian's Lord the Lord of all!

HERE break upon this cloud of chilling gloom
    Glad beams of brightness from the English sky;
    A century gone, the shades began to fly,
And make for Hope, in burdened bosoms, room.

While on the scroll of Hindoo missions gleam
    Some names, as XAVIER's,[3] three dull centuries back,
    And that of SCHWARTZ,[4] far down the lonely track,
Like single stars on Night's dark face they seem!

Not these the harbingers of India's day,
    On her old superstitions yet to dawn;
    To that diviner light our eyes are drawn,
When CAREY sailed from Albion's cliffs away.[5]

Unknown, unnoticed, in his humble sphere,
    His sacred boldness bare presumption seemed;
    And, held of some good men as one who dreamed,
His dream, like Jacob's, shines to us as clear.

In the pure light that streams o'er India now,
    Where souls, by thousands, from dumb idols turn,
    And suttee altar-fires no longer burn,[6]
Nor Ganges's tides o'er hapless infants flow.

How read we, now, the reverend critic's gibe,—
    "If but a tinker grows devout, then he
    For the far East departs infallibly"?
The parson's but the voice of scoffing tribe.

Not yet have lapsed three cycles of the sun,
    Since Sydney [7] thus the noble CAREY spurned;
    Though SOUTHEY taught — as, humbler, he had learned —
The work by "those low-bred mechanics" done,[8]

"The Bible printed in the Bengali,
    The Testament in many Hindoo tongues;"
    And honor more, that to their toil belongs,
Shall swell long annals of Eternity.

From Kettering's [9] altar England's churches caught
    The glowing flame of primal Christian days;
    Then apathy awoke to Paul-like ways,
And living Faith in Love's obedience wrought.

Across the sea the heavenly unction spread,
    And holy souls through our new Zion stirred;
    The great Command, so long unheeded heard,
Smote unstopped ears, as by the Master said.

A SCANTY score of years divides the names
    Of England's herald and of his I sing,
    In the great work to which alike they bring
Their separate zeal, yet bright with kindred flames.

I link them first, that both to India gave
    Their ardent love, and their unsullied youth;
    Strong in their zeal for that divinest truth —
From Heaven revealed, a sin-doomed race to save.

They in their single, separate toil and time,
    Clasp yet two centuries in immortal bond, —
    One to its close drawn near, and one beyond,
In sacred annals to their end sublime.

And yet, again, this noble twain as one,
    These humble lays take license bold to blend,
    As blent, unflawed, their mission in its end,
Though in broad variance of views begun.

CAREY — true heir of John the Baptist, — took
    His Lord's command without tradition's gloss,
    And through baptismal waters bore his cross,
Grateful no scant obedience there to brook.

In childhood, by involuntary rite,
    From Faith's full homage to the Master kept,
    JUDSON, in manhood's prime, his error wept,
And Faith in Love's obedience blossomed bright.

On the rude billows of the ocean tossed,
    His long default tossed more his serious mind,[10]
    Which sought not rest, but more the truth to find,
And finding, he would buy at any cost.

That cost, from his own records, we may count
    In sad disruption of fraternal ties,
    Dependent loneliness 'neath alien skies,
And blighted hopes and plans, to swell the amount.

Yet help from Heaven sustained his fainting heart,
   And conscience over interest victory won;
   High honor thus to principle was done,
In sacrifice that pierced him like a dart.

But angels strengthened him,—One from above,
   For holy deeds to Heaven's own sons are dear;
   And one of lowlier birth-place yet was near,—
His earthly angel, his in wedded love.

Mark the fair scene a Christian zayat shows
   In Bengal's capital. This exiled pair
   Receive the rite of Christian baptism there,
And Faith's pure bud in Duty's flow'ret blows.


NOW, face to face, with duty and with doubt,
   Stood the young hero on the heathen shore,
   The sponsors lost, he leaned upon before,[11]
And earthly guidance, trust and pledge without.

Yet undismayed his strong, courageous soul!
   Too much already dared and done to fear
   His Master's hand would fail of succor here;
He gave his will and way to Heaven's control.

This mute but mighty challenge, as from God,
   Found quick compliance from his native land,
   And gathered there a broad and zealous band[12]
To stay his feet in the new path he trod.

Unwelcome first, that path, to whom he left,
  Yet none might doubt his heart and lips were true;
  Not theirs, but his, the sacrifice to view;
Not they, but he, of sympathies bereft.

Nor soft resentment in their bosoms dwelt,[13]
  When soon the leading hand of God they saw;
  They owned the plan divine, without a flaw,
And gave to Heaven the grateful praise they felt.

To-day there beats no Christian heart but thrills,
  With holy joy, when his great name is breathed;
  With sacred fame his memory is enwreathed,
And Mission-History's brightest page it fills.

The hand he leaned upon was strong and true;
  He knew, as Paul had known, whom he believed;
  And, like that great Apostle, he received,
In each new trial, strength and wisdom new.

His will and way his Master's will controlled,
  And gave him Burma for his " goodly land,"
  Not Joshua clearer, by divine command,
Went and possessed fair Canaan's coasts of old.


THAT famous guild of commerce and of might,[14]
  Which swayed the Eastward Indies with its arm
  At Christian missions felt, or feigned, alarm,
And forced Heaven's messenger of peace to flight.

By foes on land and tempests on the sea,
  Through dangers and delays, in story told,
  His path was shaped, and for one end controlled,—
That he should Burma's first Apostle be.

Nor this alone reveals the hand divine,
  Seen in his tortuous course to that dark land: [15]
  Had he foregone, of his great chief's command,
That sacred rite, of saving faith the sign,

What modern John the Baptist's voice had rung
  To wake our continent from slumber's spell,
  And stir his modern followers up to tell
The story of the Cross in Burmese tongue?

What rent this young Apostle's soul with pain,
  For shattered bonds his new departure left,
  Of sweet communion with his own bereft,
And drenched his pillow with regret's sharp rain,

Yet could not move his steadfast soul to shun
  The humbling rite, at such surrenders priced,
  For that he honored less his creed than Christ,
And at the stake would do as he had done:

What filled two lands with wonder when the bruit
  Of that departure crossed the Atlantic's wave,
  Gave Burma to a baptized church to save,
And planted there a vine for gospel fruit.

WONDROUS vine with tribulations set,
   By trembling hands in unaccustomed soil,
   To human sight a waste of time and toil,
To Heaven-born Faith, pledge of vast vintage yet.

That soil had nourished, for long ages past,
   The mythic creed of Buddha, false as fair,
   Which crowns life's virtues with a dull despair,
Their sad, sole fruitage,—endless sleep at last.[16]

A system sacred in its dreams alone,
   Hoary with age and bald with barrenness;
   Lacking the touch the grave's great gloom to bless,
The hand divine, to roll away its stone.

Forbidding crimes with precepts pure, but vain,
   Dropping no balm of pardon on man's sin;
   The sad transgressor's only hope, to win
In Nigban's shadowy realm surcease of pain.

Unknown the tree save by the fruit it bears:
   And Buddha's stately stock o'er India flings
   A deadly growth of sin's revolting things,
And shapes most hateful that our nature wears.

In vain the Palm-leaves[17] noble doctrines teach,
   And Gautama's pure pattern pleads in vain;
   They fall on conscience as on rocks the rain,
No living soul is theirs men's souls to reach.

Siddartha's [18] pictured grace, on ARNOLD's page,
   By broad poetic license, he may call
   "The Light of Asia," but it shows a pall
Beneath, whose blackness deepens age on age.

Not that "the true light" shines, that every man
   Which cometh in the world may see and live;
   Lord Buddha's fabled radiance did not give
One ray of that, through all his reign we scan.

A sweet philosophy, a trancing dream,
   The poet wraps our stolen senses in;
   But waking, lo! we shudder at the sin
That blackens all the tide of Buddha's stream.

So, from the bright romance, our eyes decline
   To Paul's dark portrait of the heathen race,[19]
   Whose foul idolatries and crimes efface
All fancied beams from Asia's sky to shine.

Not twenty centuries of Siddartha's light,
   Had changed the frightful picture for its truth,
   When JUDSON on God's altar laid his youth,
With humble vow to rift that rayless night.

His vow in Heaven's great register was writ,
   And kept on earth to its supreme intent;
   Heaven's grace and power and wisdom with it went,
And through his holy zeal accomplished it.

FROM India twice expelled by its great guild,
    The wanderer found at length a resting-place,
    Less of his choice than of his Master's grace,
That His divine intent should be fulfilled.

Rangoon, on Irawaddy's silvery strand,
    And chiefest seaport of the Burman throne,
    Was site of vantage to His servant shown, —
The key to open wide his promised land:

A land beneath a fierce despotic rule,
    Where vice and rapine reigned with small restraint;
    A tyrant's grace alone to soothe complaint,
And superstition its supremest school;

A land with Nature's bounties well endowed,
    And with such charms of loveliness arrayed
    That Christian art a Paradise had made,
Which heathen priestcraft wrapped in gloomy shroud.

Rangoon, of Burma's cities earliest blest
    With JUDSON's patient prayers and toils and tears,
    Judged by the fruits of five slow circling years,
Had well his human faith alone opprest.

Through all their stress of trial and defeat,
    His heavenly trust was steadfast still and strong;
    God's promises were his continual song;
They made the roughness smooth, the bitter sweet.

GRAND PAGODA AT RANGOON.

Five years, but not of doubt, or scarce delay,
   Of daily grapple with an uncouth speech,
   (And seeking him who taught it more to teach [20])
In needful preparation sped away.

Till then the young Apostle dared not preach
   In the strange tongue he fain would make his own,
   Lest he should give the Word uncertain tone,
But by the wayside taught in simple speech.

Already, helpers on the field had come,
   To share his labors and to cheer his heart;
   And his sweet helpmate bore no meagre part,
Her feet not weary, and her lips not dumb.

Already, too, the bitter cup of grief
   Death's hand had pressed upon their shrinking lips;
   Their firstborn joy sunk in a soon eclipse,
He of their earthly solaces the chief.

AND now befell in Duty's seeming path,
   Of their sweet wedded love a trial sore;
   It may have been a gracious sign of more
That on their mutual joy should drop its scath.

Brief will I sing of what for them was long
   With doubt and dread and soothless anguish rife,
   Scarce less to him than to his tortured wife, —
His fruitless voyage, *not* to Chittagong.

To this coast-border of the Burmese land
　　He, by a chance of seldom ship, would go,
　　That there he might the state and fortunes know
Of native converts, once a mission band.

If he could find them, and their zeal renew,
　　He might the scattered handful gather soon,
　　And haply find, for service in Rangoon,
Some native helpers to their new faith true.

Ten days to go, and with the ship return —
　　With three months' happy toil to intervene,
　　And for his cause and Lord rare gains between —
His eager bosom made with ardor burn.

But now the ship another harbor sought,
　　And days were changed to weeks upon the sea;
　　And weeks to months had swelled, or ever he
Might to Rangoon again by her be brought.

He landed helpless, as for weeks he sailed,
　　His strength from famine and from fever spent,
　　Stale, sodden rice his loathly nourishment,
Till life's desire had in his bosom failed.

Scarce roused to send a pleading line ashore
　　To any English heart for " place to die,"
　　He wept, upon his knees, when help came nigh,
And friendly arms his faltering limbs upbore.

Like angels' faces, seemed to him, he said,
   Those of the Englishmen, who scarce restrained —
   When they his close and desolate cabin gained —
Their tears of pity for his woe displayed.

A soldier high in rank, but higher yet
   In soul, his every instant need supplied, —
   Raiment and nurse, and a sweet home beside,
And took his farewell soon, with love's regret.

THREE hundred miles of journey overland,
   In a palanquin borne, he reached Madras,
   Doubled defeat and pain to meet, alas!
No friendly ship to reach Rangoon at hand.

Through wasting months he wore the weeks away,
   His eyes, through weakness, for his studies vain;
   But forced inaction only tithed the pain
That wrung his tender bosom day by day.

No tidings to, or from, his love might go,
   And her suspense must sink into despair.
   My measures move to mark her sorrow where
She watched for him in vain, and watched in woe.

Since he had gone upon his ill-starred quest
   Dangers had stirred the Mission to alarm;
   A hostile viceroy menaced it with harm,
And terror deepened in her anxious breast.

Wide through the city rumors ran of war,
    And English ships sailed with the outward tide.
    The dreaded sickness raged on every side,
And rapine braved the weak restraints of law.

Her fellow-helpers from the field would fly,
    While yet an English ship might lend them wings;
    Her soul was rent with mortal shudderings
Of doubt, to flee with them or bide to die.

Her faltering will they plied to fear's consent;
    She bore her treasures with her to the ship,
    Breathed bitter farewells with a pallid lip,
And down the shining river tearful went.

For seven sad months she had no word from him;
    If yet he lived, where might she see his face?
    And Love and Duty answered, "In the place
He left thee, till thine eyes in death are dim."

Then rose her courage till her soul was great
    With innate prophecy of Oung-pen-la;
    Not yet the tardy ship had voyaged far,
And the brave woman for her lord would wait.

Back in a boat she went the second day,
    And as her soul was great, great her reward:
    At duty's post, ere long, her bosom's lord
She welcomed, and dark dangers made away.

AN era now in mission-work we mark:
    A Christian zayat [21] stands, complete and fair;
    And sole amid the Buddhist zayats there,
One heavenly lamp to shine on all else dark.

Now stated worship of the Christian's Lord
    Began beneath the blue of Burma's sky:
    Sermon and psalm and prayer, their melody
A strange sweet charm spread on the air abroad.

Ere long the truth, imbued with power divine,
    Divinely touched one heart prepared by grace, —
    First trophy of the Cross, of Burman race,
Upon the faithful Teacher's toils to shine.

What marvel that believing, yet it seemed
    To him almost too much to be believed;
    And that his patient faith that hour received
Reward of joy in measure yet undreamed?

A span of life, scarce threescore years and ten,
    Has lengthened Time's long annals of the past,
    Since Burma's rayless night was pierced at last,
And Faith received its first fruition then.

HOW shall I sing the longed-for happy day
    When Burma's first disciple of the Cross [22]
    Renounced his faith in Gautama as dross,
And put on Christ the Apostolic way?

That hallowed rite beneath a Burman sky —
  A unit only, now, of thousands more —
  Holds me entranced the happy scene before,
With joy akin to theirs who lingered nigh.

Dark on the mirror-surface of the pond,
  A shadow lay of imaged Gautama,
  Unconscious how that hour, anear and far,
Through all Rangoon and regions wide beyond,

Rang out, in the baptizer's solemn speech
  Of the high Trinity of names divine,
  The Buddha's doom, of sure though slow decline,
Far as that holy Shibboleth should reach.

Three holy names were vibrant on the air,
  First stirred that morn with Christ's baptismal rite;
  And happier vision never blessed the sight
Of three glad witnesses, triumphant there.

AS yet this band of earnest toilers moved
    Unhindered in their work of love and faith,
    Amid a thousand perils free from scath,
  As if of earth, no less than Heaven, approved.

Of Heaven's high favor in their hearts they bore
  Such strong assurance, that their hearts were strong
  To face the foes they knew must rise ere long,
As foes had met Christ's heralds oft before.

No dreams of earthly ease and gain beguiled
   Their exile and their lonely, alien lot;
   At sharp privations they would murmur not,
Nor shrink from storms of wrath and malice wild.

They watched and waited till the storm should break,
   And well divined why they had known no harm;
   While yet the hostile priests felt no alarm
For Gautama, and his proud altars' sake.

This humble man of gentle mien and ways,
   And of soft speech, though oft of import strange,
   With book and leaf could work no baleful change
In creeds and legends of the ancient days.

No secret force in Buddha's doctrines wrought,
   On their strong souls, a deep, resistless spell,
   That they should fear to have this Teacher tell
The creed of Christ, to them, with folly fraught.

So to the zayat flocked, with curious quest,
   The simple and the wise, in time and turn;
   Some to dispute, and some strange things to learn,—
The stranger still, in their own tongue expressed.

People and priest the new Apostle heard,
   With wonder some, and some his words believed;
   No more a harmless gospel so received,
Its preaching jealousy and hatred stirred.

THE viceroy's ear was moved, by hostile hint
    Of subtle charm in JUDSON's gentle speech,
    Sons of the great pagoda's courts to reach,
And reason's force must meet of power the dint.

A trifling edict from vice-regal throne
    Betrayed the secret fear the ruler felt;
    And all the city from the cipher spelt —
"Small favor to the strangers must be shown."

Then, soon, sad silence o'er the zayat fell;
    For curious feet or restless minds, no more,
    With sweet persuasion, stood its open door,
On which a vague alarm had cast its spell.

A faithful few the fearful threshold crossed,
    The new disciples at their Teacher's feet,
    In doubt, yet brave whatever ills to meet,
Or on what waves of trial to be tossed.

And now awoke within the common breast
    A nameless fear, a brooding dream of ill;
    With sense of kindling strife, stout hearts stood still,
As Nature hales her tempests in, with rest.

DEATH smites the sceptre from the monarch's hand
    As heedless of his royal rank and state,
    And theirs, no less, who in his presence wait,
As he and they were lowliest in the land.

Of late, his touch had reft the Avan throne
   Of its old King, who feared nor God nor man;
   So Buddha's altars to decadence ran,
And scanty reverence to their priests was shown.

Beneath the favor of the royal heir
   ·The great pagodas with new splendor shone,
   And the weird rites of Gautama took on
A life and vigor they had ceased to wear.

Of this new " Lord of life and death" so great,
   Who aimed the nation's landmarks to restore,
   The baffled Teacher deemed he must implore
His royal leave, Christ's Word to propagate.

Shall we, beholding Paul before earth's powers
   Uplift his Master's Cross, though they forbade,
   Chide JUDSON—with Paul's charge and armor clad —
That he restrained his zeal in these dark hours?

Of Jew or Gentile lord, no favor he,
   The fearless Tarsan, for his mission craved;
   Their haughty leave to preach the Cross he waived,
And made his path, as was his gospel, free!

He counselled not with royal flesh and blood,
   And knew no Master save his risen Lord;
   Cæsar's consent had Christ's commission flawed,
Which grander grew as by the great withstood.

Ah! not in fear the new Apostle made
   Appeal to Burma's Cæsar on his throne;
   He thought how soon his gospel might be known,
His path unbarred, the people not afraid.

DIVINER wisdom his desire denied,
   The Burman Church must grow in pain's hard soil.
   Its trophies must be won in anguished toil,
And scourges, bonds, and dungeons be defied.

So grew the ancient Church, with blood for rain,
   With flame for sunshine, and with sighs for air;
   Its sturdy strength and stature might not spare
Of crosses, and of conflicts, the rough gain.

The Cross, caressed by royal hands, had won
   O'er Burman soil a broad, but blighted, sway;
   Borne first along a steep and blood-stained way,
Its power is still of storm and not of sun.

In anxious hope, but not in craven fear,
   The Christian hero sought the heathen king,
   If haply, in the Throne's o'ershadowing,
Fruit of his toil the sooner might appear.

VAIN hope! There beamed upon "the golden face" [23]
   No smile of sufferance for the boon he sought;
   His sacred work must hence in faith be wrought,
By the sole sanction of Almighty grace.

That grace was mightier than imperial will;
   And when, from absence through a weary moon,
   He came again, in question, to Rangoon,
What had befallen him and his the while,

His heart was lifted high in joy's rebound;
   No evil hap his little flock had met;
   The faith and zeal of all were ardent yet,
And lo! new germs of life divine he found.

The wondrous energy of gospel leaven
   With silent, but resistless, power subdued,
   In heathen souls, the mystic spells of Buddh;
Shut Nigban's gates and opened those of heaven.

The Teacher's quiet ways and words of peace
   Still served to keep the waves of anger down;
   As yet they bore no menace to the crown,
And challenged no rude mandate they should cease.

Their mission and their might were like the dew,
   Which, silent and unseen, the hard soil breaks;
   Till germs invisible its touch awakes,
To bud and bloom in forms of beauty new.

Beneath the breath and dews of heavenly grace,
   Suffusing speech and smiles of lips and eyes,
   Unfolding truths as dropping from the skies,
The roots of faith in quick souls grew apace.

The gathered fruit — first cluster from the vine
   Not vainly set in Burma's unwont soil —
   Was priceless guerdon for the Teacher's toil,
And, to his faith, his Lord's approving sign.

The zayat now a perfect temple shone,
   Yet with an inward, unobtrusive light,
   (Where Nicodemus still might come by night)
With all its churchly rites and garments on.

Pastor and people, shepherd and his flock,
   Steadfast, if yet not safe within the fold,
   Kept each sweet ordinance there, as they of old,
And nigh, perhaps, as they, to bond or block.

The little church, among its new-born souls,
   Was nursing some who, taught of God, should teach.
   Thus early won the Cross from native speech,
Rills of the tide that far o'er India rolls.

O fears without, of rude disturbing foes
   And flight enforced, when — whither should he fly? —
   Add fears within of slow, fell malady,
Which pulses dearer than his own disclose!

That she should fall and fade from his fond sight,
   She who had been the day-star of his life, —
   His brave, inspiring, hoping, helping wife, —
Would leave no dawn for the succeeding night.

If he, in its deep gloom alone, could know
   What her strong soul and sweeter self had been,
   His toils of brain, and pen, and tongue between,
That depth of knowledge he would fain forego,

Or wait, — if but God willed, till it should strain
   The broader grasp of Heaven's intelligence
   To fathom that, which, to his mortal sense,
Appeared the last, impossible excess of pain.

Yet grew this dread foreboding in his soul,
   And rent his bosom with a speechless grief,
   Till, in a lesser woe there loomed relief, —
The hope that native air might make her whole.

Happy the counsel, happy his consent,
   Though she must cross alone the sundering seas;
   Duty and not delight, toils and not ease,
Their lives, so intertwined, thus rudely rent.

The noble woman, strengthened on the sea,
   Found English welcome in old England's heart;
   And gave to Christian zeal a quickened start,
In sweet exchange for Christian sympathy.

When to her native shores at length she came,
   And health's fair flush suffused her pallid cheek,
   To see that kindling glow — to hear her speak —
Set every languid Christian soul aflame!

Then manly hearts and maiden bosoms swelled,
  With holy yearnings, in her work to share;
  And threescore years can dimly yet declare
Burma's great gains of grace unparalleled.

HOW shall my song the sacred joy express
  Of her next meeting with her bosom's lord,
  Their rapture by no frowning shadow flawed,
    And mutual hope the crown of fear's hard stress?

For she had brought with her, to stay his hands,
  More laborers for the whitening harvest field,
  Known of twinned names [24] which in high honor yield
To none that star the night of heathen lands.

Great work the tireless Yüdathan [25] had wrought
  In the two weary years he toiled alone, —
  One in Rangoon, and one anigh the throne,
Where, hopeful still, the royal ear he sought.

His noblest task was in seclusion done,
  And in the shades of hostile vigilance;
  Denied by power to teach, he grasped each chance
A task to crown, of seven long years begun.

In precious fragments, year by year, his skill
  Had tuned the Testament for Burma's tongue, —
  A great work ended, and, if left unsung,
The lack my measures with default would fill.

THE Teacher at the "golden feet" had found
  Some beams of brightness from the "golden
    face,"
  And Ava offered him for dwelling-place
A royal gift, a chosen spot of ground.

A cautious gift, for which the King denied
  Its worth in gold, lest held of him, in fee,
  Later, it might a foreign freehold be, —
A thought that vexed the monarch's fear and pride.

As in some Eastern tale — for speed, 't would seem —
  " In two brief sennights " (as its angel wrote,
  And what her pen records the bard may quote)
" A home was ready there, as in a dream." [26]

A dream it was to her for three full moons;
  The fourth with more than silver filled its horn;
  Beneath its rays new dole for her was born,
And danger mingled discord with joy's tunes.

A cloud, at first no larger than one's hand,
  Spread slow abroad a shadow of alarm;
  Yet feared the Teacher to his work no harm,
While strife's sharp tremors shivered through the land.

In blind despite of Britain's conquering star,
  The Avan Emperor dared its baleful gleam;
  And proud, on Irawaddy's noble stream,
Bandoola's [27] troops flung forth the flag of war.

Meanwhile the "golden city," flushed with pride,
   To its new palace welcomed back the King [28]
   With pomps and splendors, were I fain to sing,
My graver theme the glittering scene might chide.

All Burma's princes — priest and potentate —
   Their gorgeous splendor to the pageant lent,
   Shining with rare barbaric ornament,
And jewelled emblems of their rank and state.

In gilded houdahs, borne by elephants,
   On stately steeds caparisoned in gold,
   The Empire all its dazzling glory rolled,
With blare of instruments, and priestly chants.

IN wonder, blent with hope, in his sad eyes,
   Gazed Yüdathan, and she who shared his thought
   Of that Almighty Power which they had brought,
To win this mighty Empire for the skies.

Bound — like Egyptian mummy in its swathe —
   For ages in the mythic folds of Buddh,
   And changing into evil all his good,
This nation made a fetter of its faith.

Only the hammer of the Gospel's grace
   Could smite that fetter from the Burman soul;
   O faith sublime that weapon to control,
And wake to endless life a death-bound race!

With that in hand, and closer in his heart,
    The Teacher saw the royal pageant fade,
    Nor of the crown nor threatening cross afraid,
He from the Throne would not of will depart.

How soon from smiles the "golden face" should shed
    Upon his way or work, he must remove,
    How soon from kingly grace and wifely love,
No rumor whispered that his footsteps led!

The war went on, and mission labors too,
    And one great Arm in both divinely wrought;
    And for one end, if not to finite thought,
Yet so beheld, the different dramas through.

Disaster to the boastful Burman arms,
    In Rangoon's fall, to Ava sent a shock,
    As of a stanch ship broken on a rock,
And filled the capital with wild alarms.

Suspicion on the English strangers fell,
    As spies and hostile to the Avan throne;
    And false conjectures to beliefs soon grown,
The pale-faced teachers shared the evil spell.

HERE shrinks my muse her story to pursue,
    With pains and persecutions for the verse;
    Yet should she shun their horrors to rehearse,
Her measures to their aim were half untrue.

Burma's Apostle, like the heroic Paul,
  Mockings, imprisonments, and bonds endured;
  Through wasting, weary months to pains inured —
Whose shadows darkly on my spirit fall.

Not long, or willingly, the lines shall run
  That trace, of twenty clouded moons, the tale;
  Where thought and word and metaphor must fail,
And leave the melancholy task undone.

It were an Iliad, to write with tears,
  Had not the ink of loving woman's pen
  Forbade the vain attempt to tell again,
With half her pathos, all its woes and fears.

TENDER, brave, and noble Christian soul,
  Hadst thou been less than Christian in that
    hour
  When Yüdathan was snatched by heathen power,
  From thy dear arms and thy strong love's control;

When as thou knewest — and yet did not die —
  The "spotted face"[29] of Death's stern servitor
  Had looked in his, and thy strained eyes foresaw
Not tortures only, but his death-rack nigh;

Then hadst thou sunk in that remediless swoon,
  Mercy's best succor in thine awful stead,
  Oblivious thence, and aye, since thou wert dead,
Of nameless ills for both to follow soon.

I liken thee, — I think I do no wrong, —
   At that drear dawn of every possible woe,
   To Christ's dear mother, when she saw Him go
His path of torture, shame, and death along;

She did not know, perhaps, as thou and we,
   How His poor pinioned arms her form upbore,
   And thine, "through deaths oft" (e'en as Paul's before),[80]
Till thy loved lord from threatened death was free.

I marvel less to see thee, prompt and bold,
   At the death-prison's door its captive greet,
   Crawling in pain, with fivefold fettered feet,
While fiendish guards thy nearer steps withhold.

I smile, through tears, to mark thy woman's wit,
   That triumphed o'er the cruel jailer's rage,
   And, granted use of a dead lion's cage,
Into a prison-chamber fashioned it.

The royal beast had shared a martyr's fate,
   In superstitious fear, starved till he died,
   As emblem of the British power and pride,
That threatened peril to th' imperial state.[81]

NOT seven slow months in Ava's cells of death
   Fill up the tale of woes the Teacher bore;
   It runs its horrors through, from these to more,
That chill the listener's blood and bar his breath.

The war grew fiercer with each English gain,
    And all the victories waved the meteor flag;
    Nor seemed the advance of native troops to lag,
Though everywhere their life-blood flowed like rain.

At length the valorous-souled Bandoola fell;
    He, "the Invincible," had bit the dust;
    And with him sunk, in fear, the royal trust,
As sinks the sea when breaks its mightiest swell!

As hope declined within the Emperor's breast,
    The fiendish passion of revenge took fire;
    And the pale prisoner felt its awful ire,
In woes expressed the most, when unexpressed.

A cruel, traitorous *pakan-woon* [32] had gained,
    By subtlety and fraud, the Emperor's ear;
    And plying, with false hopes, his greed and fear,
A fatal power for common woe obtained.

He with fresh-levied legions swelled war's tide,
    And tithed the ticals [83] gathered for their pay;
    His soldiers' blood stained his inglorious way,
And he, for crimes, upon the scaffold died.

The woe he wrought in power survived his doom;
    From Ava's hells to Tophet, hotter far,
    The scene is shifted now to Oung-pen-la.[34]
And horror's raven wing wears blacker gloom.

THE tender wife, whose tireless ministries,
   Though granted grudgingly by heartless guard,
   Made yet his chains and crosses seem less hard,
And could with their fond love his woes appease,

Unrecking she of sudden change, and bent,
   With woman's gentleness and tact and grace,
   To catch a ray of hope from some swart face,
She chanced to meet, as to and fro˙she went,

Bearing her nursing child upon her breast,
   One day she vainly sought him at the door;
   And learning she might see his face no more,
She sank a moment with alarms oppressed.

In one brief hour the cruel work was done, —
   Her husband snatched from her fond sight and care,
   She knew not whither, and, in sheer despair,
She sought for tidings till the set of sun.

Her eager hands might never serve him more,
   No more his food their cunning care provide;
   Her woe had been less bitter had he died,
Whate'er excess of ill and harm she bore!

When from the governor's loath lips she forced
   Tidings that set her aching heart aflame, —
   And told in some compassion mixed with shame, —
Hot, helpful torrents down her flushed face coursed.

The vengeful powers above him had decreed
  The pale-faced men, as criminals, to death;
  The sword, or flame, should rob them of their breath,
And secrecy should veil the dreadful deed.

"To Amarapoora — and its *lamine-woon*"! [85]
  From a leal servant, keeping watch anigh,
  Who caught the whisper of their doom — to die!
She won the fearful words and warning soon.

To Amarapoora, and all woes in store,
  All fears despite, her steadfast soul was drawn;
  And down the Irawaddy, with the morn,
A little skiff her exiled household bore.

Two weary leagues, and then the judge's court!
  And that, through scorching heat and stifling dust,
  With naught to buoy her burdened soul but trust
In Heaven, and hope, beneath, of false report.

AH! pains and perils, how in league they grow,
  Till "in battalions" they our fears surprise;
  Encountered, we may think, as "single spies" —
We could have met and better borne them so.

The lamine-woon had sent the prisoners on,
  And, with some milk of kindness in his heart,
  Gave the grieved household, in the clumsy cart,
A friendly "pass" to follow where they'd gone.

Then sank to depths profound Hope's radiant star,
   That erst had shone and long defied eclipse,
   As the true heroine caught from whispering lips
The ne'er-to-be-forgotten "Oung-pen-la"!

A roofless prison, falling in decay,
   And the pale victims sitting chained in pairs,
   So spent with pains that ranked their conscious cares,
It seemed their breath must cease before the day.

"*Why have you come?*" broke his mute agony,
   Deepening the terror of his soul's despair.
   No home, no refuge, and no safety there
Could the sad sufferer for his darlings see.


GRANT me, oh gentle mistress of sad song!
   Six months of unexampled woes to sing,
   In measures soft but brief. Too sharp their sting,
Too pitiful their strain, to hearken long.

*Laus Deo!* first, that from this depth of woe
   A happy mount of mercy we may climb,
   And hear the bells of God their music chime,
Behind and forward of the path we go.

A low, ill-vented room, where grain was kept,
   The weary mother made her home that night;
   And there, while six full moons fulfilled their flight,
On the rough heap of unhusked rice she slept.

She woke next morn, from God's own gift of sleep,
　　Strengthened to breast again a tide of ill;
　　Her heart and hands with added cares to fill,
And this sad tale in new distress to steep.

Upon your dainty couch, in garnished rooms,
　　Oh, Christian women who, by thousands, rest —
　　If you would have, like hers, your slumbers blest,
Pity and weep with her for heathen glooms.

Of two small Burman girls from Ava brought, —
　　Half of the scanty school she nourished there,
　　And now in all her good and ill to share, —
One, the first morn, of fell disease was caught.

To shield the other and her helpless child,
　　She bravely played the surgeon's skilful rôle,
　　Till o'er the hamlet by transmission stole [36]
The hateful ill in sequence sure but mild.

The jailer's children first her happy art
　　Bore through the malady, — scarce checked their play, —
　　And all the village through her fame made way,
So skilfully her needle played its part.

On her, alas! the evil sorest lay,
　　Upon the babe her skill was vainly spent;
　　And, hand in hand, sickness and sorrow went,
Within her cheerless chamber day by day.

ET more without than that rude cell within,
   On her strong soul there pressed a cruel grief;
   For which nor art nor love could bring relief,
Yet borne in faith as Heaven's wise discipline.

Not far from her rough bed of husk and fear,
   Beyond the prison gates her husband lay,
   In tortures she might charm, though not away,
Yet scarce to bring him food might she come near.

On the hard earth, than keeper's heart less hard,
   Nor mat nor pillow underneath him spread,
   With swollen, blistered limbs and fevered head,
And mangled, bleeding feet by fetters marred;

From his pale, wasted lips, as thus he lay,
   She heard the story of that brutal deed,
   Which none but weep in wonder as they read, —
How tyrants tore him from her sight away.

That dreadful march from Let-ma yoon's [87] fell gate,
   O'er lengthening miles of blazing sun and sand,
   Whose furnace-heat stout limbs could scarce withstand,
Was well-nigh doom to his enfeebled state.

Some gleams of Gautama's sweet charity
   Shot their rare radiance o'er that tramp of death,
   Which stopped for one poor victim his last breath,
And from his fiendish drivers set him free.

When from the mounted lamine-woon, in vain,
   The crippled Teacher humbly sought a ride,
   A Bengal servant, at his master's side,
Took instant pity on his helpless pain.

His twisted turban from his head he tore;
   Quickly in twain he rent the flowing cloth,
   And to his master and the Teacher both,
The soothing wrappers, bowing low, he bore.

Thus had Siddartha done in olden days,
   When Buddha's grace could touch the haughty soul,
   That now in lowlier bosom found control,
And from the poet's heart wins this poor praise.

About his blistered feet the cool, soft cloth
   Soothed the sharp torture of the fiery sands;
   As, leaning on a friendly arm his hands,
He dragged his feet, God's arm around them both.

THE weary days to weary weeks went on,
   And brought slight solace to the brooding woe;
   If one tide ebbed, a heavier one would flow,
Till hope of help in all but Heaven was gone.

The Teacher's eyes gained something back of light,
   As healing to his wasted limbs lent strength,
   So he could pace the prison bounds at length,
And better bear his cruel couch at night.

The tireless angel who, with feet for wings,
   About his prison hovered with her smiles,
   Won, here and there, some heart with her weird wiles,
As goodness to itself still goodness brings.

With dainty bribes and blessed acts, she bought
   What little kindnesses about her grew;
   She was so brave, so gentle, and so true,
The vileness round her gleams of beauty caught.

But her incessant toils and watchings wore
   Less her high spirit than her body frail;
   How could that in her lodging else than fail,
Where sleep came rarely, and fit food still more?

The desolate, drear hamlet met no need
   Of food or medicine, or for love or gold;
   Herself, her child, must sleep beneath the mould,
If help for both came not from Heaven with speed.

With dauntless faith in God, she charged her soul
   To hold her fainting body to her will,
   Her daring aim and purpose to fulfil,
And Ava, and her dwelling there, her goal.

TO purpose is with resolute souls to do;
   Her very weakness seemed to make her strong;
   A trinity of loves she bore along,
A Trinity, more lofty, bore her through.

At Ava, in her once dear mission-home,
    Her malady made pause enough for hope;
    Her pulse played even with Desire's broad scope,
And Fear's dark sea was flecked with sparkling foam.

Delusive hope! Like a sleep-dream it passed,
    And to the wasting illness gave new force;
    Swift, to one only end, appeared its course,
And each to-morrow seemed for her the last.

One passion now within her bosom glowed,—
    To die, where late to live, was worse than death;
    There, there alone, she fain would yield her breath,
So strong to Oung-pen-la love's current flowed.

With fevered strength she gained her medicine-chest,[88]
    And friendly drugs her faltering steps upbore
    To the great river's glistening, sun-scorched shore,
Where on a lingering boat she swooned in rest.

But still the clumsy cart-wheel blocks[89] must creep
    A league and more through tortures slow but keen;
    Across which sea of fire had she not been,
Their dirge-like groans had wrapped her in Death's sleep.

Honor we pay — and more than praise is due —
    To serving-men whose souls had suited kings;
    If shame on Burmese chiefs my story flings,
A humble Bengalee it crowns anew.

A faithful fellow he, guardian and cook, [40]
   Whose human heart rode proudly o'er his caste,
   Met her with tears, and, with alarm aghast,
Bore her frail form to its wont dreary nook.

For twenty moons, through all their wasting woes,
   No task too mean, his hands and spirit irked;
   Zealous in all, he waited, watched, and worked,
Nor saw reward, nor sought it, to their close.

MY song grows heavy with these doubled ills,
   Which lighten not as burdened weeks go by;
   But thicken, as swart clouds that choke the sky,
Till silent terror all the landscape fills.

Two months within that stifling chamber lay
   The mother's form upon the paddy heap; [41]
   Pain, weakness, and foul air forbade her sleep,
And made the night more hideous than the day.

No bread, no drop of milk, no dainty bit,
   No food but rice might the sad sufferer buy,
   Though for the famished babe the hour seemed nigh,
When Death's cold arms from hers would ravish it.

Sometimes with bribes, — and these, at times, were vain! —
   The gates would give their prisoner leave to pass;
   And then, with fetters only loosed, alas!
He dragged his feet and clanked the clinging chain.

Mark now the quest on which his steps are bent.
  His little famished child he bears around,
  If, haply, here or there, the boon be found
From some soft breast a mother's nourishment.

Thanks unto God! from Hindoo bosoms flowed
  This milk of human kindness many days;
  And for sweet strains, to mix with sombre lays,
With joy I sing this tender episode.

ETERNAL Justice sits on Heaven's high seat,
    And great doom-days to human knowledge come,
    When the black bread of crime, to its last crumb,
  The cruel wretch that moulded it must eat.

The pakan-woòn, whose malice wrought the woe
  Of the white victims sent to Oung-pen-la,
  Had stretched his foul and fiendish scheme so far
That they to Buddh's first Hell [42] by fire should go.

While yet this terror o'er their spirits hung,
  Glad tidings reached them of the traitor's death:
  The sword of Justice flashed from out its sheath,
And to the brazen Hell his soul was flung.

WHEN gloom and storm o'er land and sky have lowered,
    Until with shadow all the earth is sad,
    One burst of sunshine makes the bosom glad,
  And songs of joy from gleeful throats are showered.

Not vocal songs, but anthems of the heart,
    In deep thanksgiving rose to heaven above,
    When over Oung-pen-la God's bow of love
Gave tokens that its clouds of woe would part.

Oh blessed sign, that made the captive's chain
    Seem light as if a sudden it was broke!
    Her tender voice the blessed tidings spoke,
And rapture woke as from a dream of pain.

Deliverance came, and Yüdathan was free!
    But, after joy's sweet rain of tears, returned
    The clouds; for in the jailer's bosom burned
The hateful greed for oft-extorted fee.

"The one in chains must go, but she must stay;
    The mandate made no mention of her name."
    With bribes of stores, which late from Ava came,
This wicked obstacle was swept away.

To Ava then, but under guard-ship yet,
    The grateful group from the foul precinct went;
    She to her dwelling, but the Teacher sent
Once more to prison, where at morn they met.

He to the Burmese camp in bonds must go;
    His skill in tongues must serve the frightened King.
    Embassage now for treaty was the thing,
And he his fealty to the Throne must show.

DREAR was his voyage to the tented field,
    Cramped in an open boat 'neath chilling dews,
    With mildewed rice his only food to use,
And day and night the fickle sky his shield!

Scarce better than his prison-lot his state,
    And heavier there the fever on him fell;
    No gentle hand to soothe its fiery spell,
No smile to greet him at Maloun's war-gate.[43]

With scarce the sense or power the pen to hold,
    They forced upon him the translator's task;
    And mocked his misery, as a wilful mask,
Till a white swoon his true condition told.

Then turned their taunts and tortures into care,
    Lest Death should rap his service from their aid;
    In treaties with their conquerors to be made,
His skilful tongue and pen they ill might spare.

From stifling bamboo-hut on the scorched beach,
    They bore him, in his swoon, where he might live;
    Kind Nature proved his true restorative,
And brought him back to feeling and to speech.

His task was hard, his skill beyond a doubt,
    But doubted yet his fealty and truth;
    Ruthless to him, how dare they trust his ruth,
In the grave issues they conferred about?

His counsels, wise and just, grew soon of weight
   With the rude spirits whelmed in hopeless war,
   With foes of might and chivalry and law,
In strife invincible, as in honor great.

A SUDDEN frenzy now the camp controlled,
   And all grew white with fear as waves with foam;
   The British arms were marching on from Prome,
The "golden city" naught could save but gold.

Five million rupees [44] — the redemption fee —
   The barbarous bosom of the King appalled;
   The "strangers" to the Throne in haste were called,
And Yüdathan must lead in embassy.

But yesterday, unsignalled why or when,
   He from the camp to Ava had been sent;
   And there, by slender chance, fresh prisonment
Escaped, and that at Oung-pen-la again.

The governor of the city's northward gate,
   With friendly zeal, the highest court besought,
   Himself as surety gave, and home he brought
His captive guest, the King's high will to wait.

It was for Burma, as for JUDSON, well
   That slender chance was in the hand of God;
   Man's rude mistake was His directing rod;
What we count trifles His great ends foretell.

The Teacher, keeping his sole work in view,
   And well forecasting what the end must be,
   Shunned, with avail, the hopeless embassy,
And for another stood his hostage true.

AGAIN the finger of the Lord behold!
   For weeks that only face he had not seen,
   Which in his woes his light from heaven had been,
Nor of her weal or woe had he been told.

The moon's white rays fell softly on her gate,
   As he was hurried, pleading vainly, past,
   Nor tears, nor threats, nor bribes, availed at last,
One golden moment for love's sake to wait.

Could he have glanced within that dear abode,
   His heart had falsely played his faltering feet,
   To see what there his shrinking eyes must meet, —
A sight denied, to God's sweet mercy owed.

Spared from the embassage, he like a bird,
   With wounded wing for wonted flight half free,
   His mangled feet let not, at speed, to flee,
He went, 'twixt hope and fear, from vague hint heard.

His door stood wide, as where might welcome be,
   Yet no sweet voice gave greeting to his ear;
   A Hindoo nurse and a wan child, to fear
O'er hope within his breast gave victory.

Beyond, oh, fearful veil to lift ! she lay
  As one not sleeping, but from terror dead ;
  Close-shaven locks and ghastly features said,
"Sickness and abject want have had their way."

Love, that despair and death might vivify,
  A moment bowed above the prone, white form ;
  A sighing breath, a tear with that love warm,
Fell on the wasted face, and Death passed by !

Oh, miracle of love, by Heaven endowed,
  Which conquered Death at moment so supreme !
  She woke, as one who starts from horrid dream,
Or day-star bursts from foldings of black cloud.


CAME, with the envoys, slight encouragement,
  In easier terms the hundred lacs [45] to pay, —
  A fourth part, promptly, at twelve days' delay,
And, with the sum, all English captives sent.

The British general strict requirement made
  For "the good Teacher, with his wife and child ; "
  At which the King, with speech and manner mild,
His selfish wish and crafty mind betrayed :

"They are not English people ; they are mine ;
  I will not let them with the English go : "
  Vain speech with which to meet victorious foe,
And vainer still to thwart the Will divine.

A bold adventurer, of vague renown,
  Had to renewed defiance stirred the King:
  "If he to Pugan might an army bring,
He'd make impregnable that ancient town.

"There would he meet, and there the foe destroy;"
  His gods had made him mad for his own doom,
  And madness in the King's vexed breast found room,
Such reckless means and leader to employ.

With flaunting banners went the legions out,
  And the old city swiftly fortified;
  Scarce slower smote the English arms her pride,
And put the "golden city's" last resource to rout.

Before the King the braggart stood again,
  Asking new troops the battle yet to wage;
  The angry monarch, hot with shame and rage,
Consigned him to the headsman to be slain.

The crafty King, in hope his vengeance might
  Be veiled from English eyes, made grave pretence
  That he was slain for disobedience
To his command, "the English not to fight."

MEANWHILE the patient victors slowly drew,
  But steadfast still, the "golden city" nigher;
  The King's delay provoked the leader's ire,
Though peace, and not assault, he kept in view.

Yet new ambassadors in hope were sent,
   To soften, still, surrender's bitter price;
   Their answer was dismission in a trice,
And warning notes of peril imminent.

Alarm, to terror, through the city ran;
   Palace and people shared alike the spell;
   With one consent and haste incredible,
They brought their treasures to the melting-pan.

Vessels and gauds of silver and of gold,
   To sate the fervid flame, flowed fast and free;
   The King and Queen the work watched eagerly,
And soon, in weight, the needed sum was told.

The native mind, by its own morals bound,
   Feared, and forbore, in English truth to trust;
   The King and Court, themselves of mould unjust,
Knew not where right and honor might be found.

They would not send, at once, the gathered tax:
   Fearing lest that and many captives gone,
   The foe would move the royal city on —
They sent, of all the treasure, six sole lacs.

The "sacred Teacher" they constrained to go,
   To help their plea, though he declared it vain;
   The ill-judged gold to Ava came again,
With large forbearance from the advancing foe.

" If but the full instalment of the sum
    Reached them, ere they the city's outposts reached,
    Their word of honor should be unimpeached,
Nor to the 'golden city' harm should come."

Persuasive words, by conquering banners backed,
    Dark prison-doors upon their hinges turned;
    To Oung-pen-la the fire of freedom burned,
The terms of peace nor souls nor rupees lacked.

LAUS DEO, yet! On Irawaddy's breast,
    A mild March moon its silver splendor poured
    Upon a fleet of golden war-boats moored
About a shallop noted from the rest.

Upon its deck stood Yüdathan erect,
    His happy eyes alternate, lift and low,
    Now to glad heaven, now, with its light, to go —
Where stood his angel in earth's garments decked.

Free and united! They, for moons a score,
    Had known no day that was not dark with dread;
    Now, with the terror from their bosoms fled,
Which quivered like gay ripples on the shore.

Above them England's royal banner waved;
    Each fold and color of the symbolled cloth
    Bore pledges, sweet and eloquent to both,
That they from danger, as from death, were saved.

The rapture of that strange, moonlighted sail
  Was to their senses type of heaven's own bliss;
  Time had no equal antepast of this,
Till mortal in immortal breath should fail.

THE British camp! In the sweet morning light
  What leaden shadows from their hearts were gone;
  What mystic radiance from the white tents shone,
River and earth and sky changed in a night!

See now, from off the flag-environed shore
  In bannered boat a stately escort comes,
  And o'er the glancing waves, the roll of drums,
To greet the happy captives, free once more!

What honors might be paid to rank and state
  By English arms, in Victory's jubilant hour,
  Fell on their humble heads in affluent shower,
Themselves, in goodness and in suffering great.

Fast flew a fortnight by on balmy wings, —
  Sweet days of honor, courtesy, and rest, —
  To swell with thankful joys the throbbing breast
Tortured so late with tyranny's sharp stings.

One day a splendid banquet was prepared,
  In honor of the royal treaty made,
  While yet the Burman deputies delayed.
Nor glittering pomp nor pageantry was spared.

The camp with gold and crimson flags was hung;
   A hundred cannon thundered on the air;
   And mirth and music rang out everywhere,
While songs of victory and peace were sung.

When the gay feasters to the banquet went,
   They marched in couples to the music's tone,
   But the commander, at the front, alone,
Till all were halted at a curtained tent.

There, while the Burmans looked with vague surprise,
   The general stepped the snowy tent before,
   And from its light veranda, through the door,
Vanished a moment from their curious eyes.

Emerging then, a lady on his arm,
   He seated her beside him at the head;
   While dusky faces there turned pale, or red,
With conscious shame or deathly white alarm.


A LITTLE comedy enacted there
   Came nigh to marring English courtesy:
   " Old friends of yours I fancy these must be,"
Said the gay host, aloud, to lady fair.

Her smile from further speech her lips excused;
   But he, " You must have treated that one ill;
   See how his forked beard is quivering still."
Then she, — half pitiful and half amused, —

"His memory troubles him, perhaps. Too well
   The Burman knows me, and may fitly fear
   Ill to himself, that you protect me here;
In English I a little tale may tell:

"When Yüdathan in Avan prison lay,
   Five cruel fetters on his ankles fast,
   I, fearing that each day would prove his last,
To that man's dwelling made my weary way.

"A weary time — from morn till noon — denied,
   He heard at length my prayer, and that forbade;
   A silken sunshade in my hand I had,
And he, with rudeness, snatched it from my side.

"In vain I pleaded, to his cruel ear,
   My need of shelter from the scorching sun,
   And in its stead besought a paper one;
But his loud laughter mocked my trembling tear."

A burst of honest anger from the lips
   Of gallant officers was ill restrained;
   Their kindling eyes the English text explained
To him, whose joy it cast into eclipse.

Her gentle heart felt sooth for his wild fear,
   Which stood in pearls upon his tawny face;
   And with an angel's heart and woman's grace,
In soft Burmese she bade him nothing fear.

She had endured so long, from ribald tongue
  And savage breast, coarse gibes and cruelties,
  That she had gained the grace to liken these
To jewels in her heavenly necklace hung.

Her voice and smile the wave of passion broke,
  And brought again the glow of festal mirth;
  But in that voice and smile the woman's worth
To some strong men a new evangel spoke.

The Christian Teacher, witnessing the scene,
  Was moved to own it " passing rich in mirth;"
  His Master, had He walked with him, on earth
Was yet so human, He too might have been.

HER self, her story, and her sufferings won
  Homage from men, as if she came from heaven,
  In whose stout hearts she left a little leaven,
Whose sacred working may outlive the sun.

The noble chief who ruled at Yandabo,
  Himself most honored that he honored her,
  And him not less to whom to minister
She let, in love, no least occasion go —

CAMPBELL, Sir Archibald, of Burman fame,
  More honor in the ages yet shall win,
  For that, in love, he took the JUDSONS in,
And linked with theirs his prowess and his name.

With tears of joy his fostering camp they gained,
   And paid their praises there to Heaven's high grace;
   Their tears of sorrow rained upon the place
When Duty, to depart, their feet constrained.

Laden with blessings, and by true hearts loved,
   Their way from perils shielded to Rangoon,
   'Mid love's lost toils the song will find them soon,
From camps of woe and weal alike removed.

Maloun and Yandabo! two names to stand
   To them, of all life's possible extremes,
   Types wide apart as foul and happy dreams,
Now terrors and now raptures to command.

RANGOON no more repaid their sacred toils;
   Their mission-house a heap of ruins lay,
   The little church was scattered in dismay,
And all around them War displayed its spoils.

For Pegu-an troops beleaguered now the town,
   Intent the independence to regain
   Of their old province, held in subject chain
Forged by Alampra's [46] prowess and renown.

Lost ground and hopes defeated could not turn
   Their hearts from Burma and their holy cause;
   Crossed here by tumults and oppressive laws,
For whiter harvest-fields their bosoms yearn.

The Teacher at the British camp displayed
   Such skill and aptness in diplomacy, —
   While none could use the Burman speech as he, —
That its brave general coveted his aid.

The Avan King, too, knew his worth so well,
   He fain at court had kept him as "his own,"
   And with rewards and honor, from the throne,
Had urged him at his capital to dwell.

Not honors and not gold the Teacher sought;
   The boon he craved the monarch would not grant,
   His royal grace through Burma's realm to plant
The new religion from the New World brought.

Forbidden this, the "golden city" lured
   No more the Teacher's heart to linger there;
   Burma had other fields as Ava fair,
In which soul-liberty might be secured.

THE peace but now confirmed at Yandabo,
   Of southern provinces the Empire robbed;
   And after these his eager bosom throbbed
As gospel-fields to reap, if first to sow.

On the east border of the Bengal Bay,
   The ceded province of Tenasserim
   Another "promised land" appeared to him,
For safe possession under Christian sway.

Already he had viewed the province o'er,
　　With England's envoy, to appoint the place
　　Which its new capital might fitly grace,
Of Amherst named, close on the Salwen shore.

There the new mission station soon was set,
　　And there his loved ones found an English home;
　　While he, on errands grave and great, should roam,
Close knit with his unfaltering purpose yet.

Only, for that he might make more secure
　　For him and others Burma's gospel-field,
　　Would he his strength to earthly service yield,
His loyalty to Christ, so great, so pure.

Rewards at Ava and at Yandabo,
　　For embassies and toils of pen and speech,
　　Might well, in sum, a hundred times outreach
What golden rills from mission-work would flow.

So keen and lucent was his sense of right,
　　He for himself could hold nor gifts nor fees,
　　Received beyond his sacred ministries,
And keep the honor of his service white.

Into the mission treasury hence he told [47]
　　The generous gains his civic service won;
　　And if some thought he had to duty done
No violence, to call his own that gold,

A higher law his conscience and his deed,
   For highest service, with effect declared ;
   The mission counsellors his judgment shared,
And made his deep conviction thence their creed.

RELUCTANT now and slow my measures move,
   Tender and mournful, to the place of death ;
   Where so great loveliness resigned its breath,
A threnody of woe the song must prove.

She who, at Ava and at Oung-pen-la,
   Won brutal men to softness by her grace,
   Illumined prison glooms with her sweet face,
And on despair shone like a morning star ;

She who for hopeless hunger yet found food,
   Whose touch on anguish dropped a soothing balm,
   Whose voice was music, and her sigh a psalm,
Whose presence shamed all sin by her pure good,—

She in the fulness of a fresh delight,
   Of hope rekindled from its ashes cold,
   And ere her sainted life was growing old,
Took to her spirit's native home her flight.

She died without the farewell clasp and kiss
   Which would have soothed the agony of death ;
   He was not near to catch her lapsing breath,
Or charm its sigh into a living bliss.

ANN HAZELTINE JUDSON

Alone with God, for peace to her sweet soul,
   (Though kindly care and willing hands were nigh)
   It had not been so hard for her to die,
If in his arms had " broke the golden bowl."

He filled her thought until she thought no more;
   Her latest words were left, to nerve his heart,
   From mission-labors never to depart,
Till she should meet him on the heavenly shore.

When one half more the sun had run his round,[48]
   The child-bud fading while upon her breast,
   Had withered quite, and, laid with her at rest,
Made doubly dear the Hope-tree shadowed ground.

O honored husband, teacher, friend, and love!
   Was ever mortal more of earth bereft?
   'T was well of Heaven thou hadst thy Master left,
And saintly eyes on watch for thee above!

A YEAR at Amherst sped, and then Maulmain;
   For men propose, but God is arbiter;
   It pleased the English general to prefer
The latter place to plant his camp again.

Thither the tide of life and motion flowed,
   And dear to him as was the Hopia-tree, —
   A spot for sweet and hallowed memory, —
The Teacher made Maulmain his fixed abode.[49]

There centred long the hopes, the toils, the prayers,
  Which crowned with blessing there, knew yet no bound,
  To which the tocsin of the Cross might sound,
To save the perishing from Satan's snares.

Two years of war and bonds and wanderings,
  By hostile hands delayed, by strange winds blown,
  His first fruits scattered, little new seed sown —
Appeared a day of small and feeble things.

His steadfast faith alone, in Him whose voice
  Had sent him forth with promise of His aid,
  Made him, in front of perils, unafraid,
And in deep tribulations to rejoice.

And with the mystic glass of faith for sight,
  The small things into new proportions grew;
  Could he but see their thronging shadows through,
The instant glooms might kindle into light.

The broken zayats could be built again,
  The scattered church had living pillars yet;
  And wasted months, that waked his keen regret,
Seen as his Master sees, seem fit as few.

Money and men the growing cause required;
  And through our land the Macedonian cry
  Which Paul, from Troas, drew to Philippi,
From Burma rang, and Christly souls inspired.

Nor rang the cry in vain; and JUDSON's hands,
   Like those of Moses, on the hill, were stayed
   By BOARDMAN, the beloved, and faithful WADE,
Whose names are shrined throughout all Christian lands.

The laborers were so few, so great their need,
   The zealous converts into teachers grew;
   And to their mission and their Master true,
They went with zeal to sow the gospel seed.

The sowers cast it oft on stony ground;
   For Sin and Superstition, hand in hand,
   With foul idolatries filled all the land,
And precious fruit, though rare, made joy abound.

The Maulmain zayats gathered eager throngs,
   Some to dispute, and more "new things" to hear;
   While daily some, with eyes and hearts sincere,
Gave heed to gospel sermons, prayers, and songs.

  RESTLESS zeal now filled the Teacher's mind
   New centres of the gospel truth to form;
   Fain would he take Sin's citadels by storm;
For that, his earthly all he had resigned.

His loved ones he had laid 'neath Burman sod,
   His honored sire now slept within the tomb;
   For what in his lone bosom was there room
But single, sacred, ceaseless zeal for God?

That he might come by heavenly gains secured,
   In heathen souls to Christ from idols won,
   To count his earthly sacrifices none,
And naught the bonds and pains he had endured.

Why wonder we that such devotion grew
   In the great, empty chamber of his soul,
   To mystic passion taking there control,
And moulding his rare nature half anew?

To mien and manner of a charming grace,
   And social powers to make his presence sought,
   Which shone the more for halo of high thought,
He joined the spell of pathos in his face.

To veil such suavity with sombre air,
   And smile, as if to smile 't were his no more;
   To shun, to others' pain, their festal door,
And where delights were few, refuse a share,—

All this in him was fruit of lengthened pain,
   Which wounded not his gentle flesh alone,
   But haply into sickness of the brain had grown,
So deep had bitten in his soul the chain.

Upon the street or in the zayat, met
   Of priest to cavil, or of carl to learn,
   His drooping eye with its old fire would burn,
And his young zeal and force shine vital yet.

Unstinted every work of sacred aim;
  He preached and wrote and toiled and went,
  Afar and near, till oft his strength was spent
In service, or in sacrifice, the same.

WITH closer copy of his Master's mode
  Than it were wise, or well, for all to make,
  He sought the jungle for that Master's sake,
And in its glooms for forty days abode.

If wingèd angels bore him there no aid,
  Sweet ministers of grace his needs supplied;
  And when, in deeper glooms, he fain would hide,
A strange lone spot his place of prayer he made.

Near where a moss-grown Buddhist temple stood,
  A tall pagoda, desolate and grim,
  A haunt more fit for ravenous beasts than him,
And a drear distance in the jungle-wood.

There, in rude oratory, day by day,
  In meditation deep, and prayer devout,
  From all the world and worldly things shut out,
The Christian hermit passed long hours away.

When shadows o'er his altar fell, at length,
  He sought the hermitage his hands had reared
  On the thick jungle's edge, the town that neared,
Where sleep and pilgrim's bread sustained his strength.

An aged man who at his feet had sat
   Tracked once unseen his Teacher's jungle-way;
   And the next dawn, when he was come to pray,
O'er a rude bench was twined of twigs a mat.

If yet he knows who that dear deed had done,
   He learned it where all knowledge is — above;
   An old disciple thus had shown his love,[50]
Renewed ere long in realms beyond the sun.

PASSED thus some months of his devoted life,
   A part exceptional which some might deem,
   In its subjectiveness of aim extreme,
   An unwont term of inward passionate strife.

A struggle, rather, shaped by his great zeal,
   Through years of self-surrendering toils and pains,
   To grasp beyond and garner priceless gains,
Of heathen souls their everlasting weal.

That holy zeal, like mountain stream close pent
   In unwont bounds, that breaks opposing walls,
   And from its rush and turmoil silent falls,
Self-centred, motionless, in force o'erspent;

Baffled by foes and bruised by fetters sore,
   Wounded to weakness, at the brink of graves,
   Rent its restraints to sink in lapsing waves,
And find, within itself, its flood and shore.

If overwhelmed with heavy stress of grief,
   His ardent nature sunk beneath the wave,
   Till he communed too closely with the grave,
And in monastic vigils sought relief,

He from the spell to brighter zeal awoke,
   Forgot the open grave [61] — until he died —
   And, by his dreams, his labors multiplied,
Till gospel light o'er hills and valleys broke.

ON Burma's borders, north and south and east,
   Range numerous hill-tribes simple and uncouth;
   And, chiefly on the mountains of the south,
He spread for the Karens the gospel feast.

Untamed and shy, from towns they kept aloof,
   Save when to enter them by needs constrained;
   Nor to their haunts was easy access gained, —
Groups of rude huts of wood and branch-wove roof.

At Rangoon, first, the Teacher saw these men,
   By twos or threes, go straggling by his door,
   In a strange garb he ne'er had seen before,
But, with his eye, his heart they captured then.

Of his own converts eagerly he sought
   All that he might of the strange tribe to learn;
   His blessed mission was too broad to spurn
The sons of men, how rude soe'er their sort.

Not yet they knew the power of gospel grace,
  Though in their bosoms glowed its heavenly hope;
  To their dim sight they lay beyond its scope,
A wild, intractable, and hopeless race.

It fell, in time of war, in Rangoon lay
  A wild Karen held bond-slave for a debt,
  The Teacher's questions well remembered yet
Led a disciple there the debt to pay.

His bondman then, as custom made the rule,
  He held till time and peace enabled him,
  In the freed province of Tenasserim,
To bring the debtor to the Christian school.

There Ko-Thah-byu the one Great Teacher found,
  And to his countrymen the Christ made known;[52]
  In other waiting hearts the good seed sown
Made heathen jungles bloom as gospel ground.

YET slow the precious germs of truth to spring
  In souls by gross idolatries long slaved;
  And by revolting vices more depraved,
Strong to their sins, for sin's own sake, to cling.

Of triple tours along the jungle streams
  That join their currents to blue Salwen's tide,
  And oft, afoot, to villages aside,
Like some strange tale the Teacher's record seems.

True, yet its truth than fiction stranger reads, —
    A small boat's company on conquest bent,
    Without a flag or warlike instrument,
A pale-faced officer his forces leads;

Hostile to none they meet, and yet at strife
    With the false gods before whose shrines they kneel,
    Their only weapons words and strong appeal
To turn their paths of Death to ways of Life.

And some they won to tears, and some to wrath
    At the divine requirement to repent,
    As fearless Paul to old Galatia went,
And starred with Christian churches all his path.

Burma's Apostle in the jungles taught,
    And whom, in love, his sweet evangel prized,
    Or old or young, believing, he baptized,
So mightily by him God's spirit wrought.

Thus, here and there, through all the wilderness
    Gleamed gospel lamps upon the heathen gloom,
    Like twinkling stars before the ampler room
The risen sun shall, at God's noon-time, bless.[53]

Who is so wise the heart's intent to tell?
    With bitter oft is dashed the cup of sweet;
    Tares evermore are mingled with the wheat,
As witnesses the Master's parable.

When on his path defection cast its gloom,
   He would not keep the record from his page;
   And when his way was blocked by Buddhist rage,
Not more his pen than fell his heart afraid.

As if with tears for ink, his pleas were writ
   For men and means the spreading fields to reap,
   Alike when blighted prospects made him weep,
And when the smile of God the darkness lit.

NOW may a happy marriage song be sung,
   When two lone hearts their widowhood forsake,
   And in love's hallowed bonds fit union make,
Where double griefs their shadows long had flung.

With three slow years of sacred, sweet employ,
   Had sainted BOARDMAN's widow crowned his tomb,
   And kindled light from Heaven 'mid heathen gloom
In scores of Karen hearts at old Tavoy.

Her holy heroism matched with JUDSON's well:
   One only aim each earnest soul inspired;
   And his great heart, with whelming conflicts tired,
Found rest and life again in Love's strong spell.

A decade of redoubled zeal ensued
   In mission-labors wider and more wide,
   Harvests with harvesters were multiplied,
And the Great Husbandman pronounced them good.

When five long lustrums of his life had passed
   In work that seemed half wasted for small gains,
   So scarred it was with hindrances and pains,
Its high achievement we behold at last!

Five years of wrestle with a crude, quaint speech
   Had shaped it deftly to his tongue and pen,
   And twenty more availed for millions then —
To place God's Holy Book within their reach.

How great that toil in doing could we guess,
   By all its bars and barrenness of aid,
   As bricks, aforetime,[54] without straw were made,
Yet must it seem immeasurably less

In what was done, in the accomplished deed —
   Unnumbered open leaves spread all abroad,
   With messages of grace and peace from God
That every hungering eye and heart might read.

What were the Palm-leaves in the Baskets more
   Which Buddha's sun-robed priests alone could spell,
   When every man might make his sick soul well
With healing leaves of grace unknown before?

This marvellous work, if seeming long deferred,
   Had shown its steps through all the tedious way;
   Each printed tract of millions, yet a ray
Of light divine to illume the spoken word.

That great work wrought — the Burman Bible done —
  Stands like some Pharos 'twixt two eras built ;
  Its backward light quenched in unfathomed guilt,
Its forward gleams outstretching to God's sun !

O priests of Buddh, your triple baskets bear,
  And plunge them with their mystic palm-leaves forth
  On Irawaddy's tide ! Gone is their worth,
And vain their symbols as the empty air.

TWIXT Burma's capital and port half-way
  Lies Prome, a city populous and old,
  Where one brief season through, with spirit bold,
The Teacher strove foundations new to lay.

His soul was sore that into Burma's heart
  He might not cast the precious gospel seed,
  And, near its golden Throne, with pagans plead
From idol shrines and worship to depart.

If now at Prome, on the great river's marge,
  Some heavenly grain in patience he might sow,
  His tears, more potent than the flood's strong flow,
Might the small seed in germs of grace enlarge.

Lodged in an English home — all else denied —
  A ruined zayat he his temple made,
  Which, scarce beyond a tall pagoda's shade,
Should lure its votary's steps to turn aside.

His face and dress, his voice and open book,
　　As in Rangoon, the curious passer drew,
　　And daily some returned, while daily grew
The throng to listen, or content to look.

Hope in his heart now mounted into flame;
　　No threatening tones the hush of hearing stirred,
　　While in soft Burman speech he preached the Word,
And some eyes gleamed with joy, or sunk with shame.

Thus glided days away, till one sad morn
　　The Teacher in his zayat sat alone;
　　Cold looks or shy toward the door were thrown,
As if of sudden apprehension born.

Counsel, if not command, from Ava came,
　　That he should turn his face and feet from Prome;
　　His mission there might find no favoring home,
And in his tortured bosom sank Hope's flame.

Yet bravely oft the heathen zayats near,
　　And most on rite and funeral days, he preached,
　　Where few, or many, by his words were reached,
If haply he might win some willing ear.

AT a great idol's side, beneath its roof,
　　One Burman worship-day, a brick his seat,
　　He preached the Cross close at the idol's feet,
And with soft utterance silenced fierce reproof.

His native helpers — three young Burmese men —
   Echoed their leader's zeal with earnest word,
   And Moung Dway's native eager tones he heard
Ring out the other side the idol then.

At length the work, begun in hope, must close
   In seeming failure to our human sight,
   And proud old Prome be left in heathen night,
Whenas faint gleams of gospel dawn arose.

Not yet in Burma, 'neath its native King,
   Might a still kinglier lordship be proclaimed;
   Not yet, of gods of brick and stone ashamed,
Her swarthy sons to Christ would homage bring.

Now may we list his words at that sad hour,
   To Maulmain and Rangoon and Boston sent,
   Upon the week's last day, and that nigh spent,
His sinking soul sustained by Heaven's high power.

He and his three disciples were afloat
   Upon the golden river's wrinkling tide;
   Rich sunset glories gilded old Prome's pride,
Her god Shway-San-dau [55] gleaming on their boat:

"Farewell, old Prome; farewell, thy towering god,
   ·Against whose spell if I have vainly striven,
   As yet too firm thy base-stones to be riven,
Soon shalt thou fall, smit by Jehovah's rod.

" Of those who gild thee with thy splendors now,
   And pay their senseless homage at thy court,
   The sons shall of thy tinselled towers make sport,
And thy tall head prone to the dust shall bow.

" Farewell, oh Prome ! Thy pagan sons, farewell ;
   Here I had fain my life's last labors spent.
   Ye ask me not to stay, and I am sent
Where I the story of the Cross may tell.

" I leave ye gospel tracts, and pray ye read ;
   And if ye call me, though in whispered voice,
   At Burma's farthest bounds, I will rejoice,
And on the wings of love come back with speed ! "


IN wise retreat, yet in no timid flight,
   The envoy of the Cross from peril goes ;
   Less his, than his exalted Master's foes
Engird him with their fierce tyrannic might.

Within the Emperor's gates he lingers yet,
   And at Rangoon his standard lifts anew ;
   With tireless zeal his labors to pursue,
And with fresh trophies soothe his old regret.

Month after month his house a zayat proved,
   By eager feet and hungry hearts beset ;
   Demands for Gospel leaves could scarce be met,
Though to all haste the Maulmain press was moved.

Besides the Gospels and the " Scrippet " leaves [66]
    (These latter single texts, or two or three,
    Like a sole leaf from off a spreading tree,
Whose scantiness the weary traveller grieves),

A score of tracts, with skill and care prepared —
    Appeal and argument and proof, designed
    To reach and win the subtle native mind —
In the great gospel work had largely shared.

Honor to minds and pens of love inspired,
    Of men and women on the mission field,
    This verse were bare and blameful not to yield
For vital helps in the great cause required.

With ardent clamor, sometimes urged with tears,
    When scanty grew the Teacher's hoarded store,
    And unavailing his strong pleas for more,
Came suitors from afar 'twixt hopes and fears.

The " View," the " Balance," and the " Catechism,"
    Poor Bennet's press toiled day and night to print;
    Hoe's " patent " then had been to him a mint,
These tracts to coin for all the land's baptism!

HIS double toils, unintermitted still, —
    Toils with his pen, and wayside counsels more, —
    Upon his shattered nerves incessant bore,
And wasted only not his iron will.

The mission guardians and the Church at home
   Yearned to behold their great Apostle's face,
   The rest for him — for them the inspiring grace —
And sent him love's strong summons while at Prome.

True servant to his Master's work, and more
   Stern martyr to his own most tender heart,
   That ne'er from Maulmain's harbor might depart
An English ship, or bound to his own shore,

That brought not his deep longings to his eyes,
   To dim the vision — sweeter still for tears —
   Of scenes and faces of his childhood's years,
Whose sweet remembrance symbolled Paradise.

And here we read, through tears to his akin,
   His strong heroic answer to the call, —
   "I lay my heart's desire 'neath Duty's pall,
Content, from toils, God's rest to enter in."

Great-souled, he spared himself nor toils nor pains,
   Yet cared and watched, with tenderness and zeal,
   For all his fellow-helpers' want and weal,
His happiest guerdon in their happiest gains.

When faithful BOARDMAN in the jungles died,
   His holy armor girt upon his back,
   His brother-heart was broken on the rack
Of woe, with Christ's for Lazarus allied.

The Mission was his heart's intensest throb;
  Its life-blood intermingled with his own;—
  All else resigned, he lived for that alone—
His daily breath, a sigh of prayer, a sob.

WHEN to full fifty years his life had run,
  And half of these on Burman soil were spent,
  His eye and heart in retrospect were bent
What he had seen, and what his Lord had done.

He saw with half dismay his ten years' toil
  In Burma's seaport blighted and undone,
  Scattered afar the little flock he won,—
Of persecution and of wars the spoil.

He saw of Ava and of Oung-pen-la
  The dreadful prisons and their galling chains;
  And in his feet could feel the lingering pains,
As Paul before him bore his Master's scar.

He saw the graves of Hope, the graves of Love,
  In deeper shade than of the Hopia-tree;
  But on the "golden face" he might not see
The smile he sought, his mission to approve.

Ah! many clouds upon his backward sight
  The eager, brave, and faithful Teacher saw;
  In all his earnest toils defect and flaw
Shed, for his eye alone, a dubious light.

His heart a happier retrospection gained,
   As deeper, farther than his eye its glance
   Beneath, beyond the instant circumstance,
And upward into Heaven's pure radiance, strained.

Therein the ruin at Rangoon was robed
   With softening vestments of Divine intent;
   Each harm and hindrance there in wisdom sent,
To prove and crown his faith by trials probed.

And to his heart the fetters did not reach,
   That to his flesh seemed more than he could bear;
   The light from Heaven revealed his Master there,
With " It is I, be not afraid " — His speech.

And when upon the Hope-tree graves his heart
   Looked, lo! the shadows all had fled;
   He saw at God's right hand those who were dead,
And turned from death no more his gaze apart.

And, with new vision, seeing what was done,
   His introspect his bosom filled with peace;
   Doubts, fears, and cankerous sorrows knew surcease;
And Burma's night broke in Christ's rising sun.

New mission-posts beneath a friendly flag,
   If only on the Empire's marge, are set,
   And in the reach of Ava's subjects yet,
While gospel lamps flame forth on crest and crag.

Beyond the Teacher's fondest hopes at first,
  That he might count for Christ a hundred souls,
  Lo! to a tenfold reach his record rolls
Of bonds of sin and superstition burst.

Karens, Taligns,[57] and Burmans to the Cross
  From Buddhist idols and pagodas turn,
  And kindling fast the signal lanterns burn,
Where Christian zayats jungle-glades emboss.

Nor these sole trophies of five lustrums shine;
  The Book of God ten thousand natives read,
  And every verse a blow to Buddha's creed,
If but God's Spirit breathes along the line.

Fairer than leaves of lotus and the palm
  Spring leaves of love for guilty pagan souls,
  Where Salwen's stream, or Irawaddy rolls,
And lo! the sin-sick seek their healing balm.

FROM backward outlook, thus with gladness crowned,
  The vision changes, in life's wonted way,
  To one of shadows veiling sunny day,
As 'neath sky-kissing hills dim vales are found.

The iron rusts, the heart of oak decays,
  Though long defied of each are strain and storm;
  And wasting ills assail the virile form,
Whose tempest-scars we look on with amaze.

His voice, mellifluous and magnetic, fell
   To painful whispers ominous and hoarse;
   And dreading deeper malady and worse,
Along the paths that guard life's citadel,

He sought the sooth and vigor of the air
   That borrows balm and blessing from the sea;
   Nor that, nor draughts of Christian sympathy
At Serampore, wrought of the wrong repair.

Not long enough at sea, nor lingering long
   Where duties gave him intermissions sweet,
   More eager loved ones at his home to greet,
The voyage closed in fear, as so this song.

HOPE sprang again as now the year declined;
   And one sweet Sabbath morn his longed-for voice
   In Maulmain's zayat made sad souls rejoice,
While happy Burmese eyes like planets shined.

His public labors lessened, steadier grew
   His arduous work on Burma's unwont speech,
   Its subtlest sense and idioms strange to reach,
With rare acumen and perception true.

His printed Bible yet must be revised;
   No needless shade must cloud that Lamp of Life.
   With pain and weakness often now at strife,
Each precious moment for that toil he prized.

With this grand century's fourth decade begun,
  The master-piece of his achievement stands,
  A work in all its parts of mortal hands,
For earth and Heaven, as of archangels, done.

Now darken mists and glooms his onward way,
  Yet not his faith's exalted reach obscure;
  As earthly joys recede Heaven's grow more sure,
And gild the cloud's dark crest with rainbow ray.

Again the sea, and far its waves to cross,
  Counselled of all, he dallied with delay;
  Counting the cost and greatness of the way,
He let occasion slip, and felt the loss.[58]

A fortnight to Bengal, and its fourth day
  Stranded the stately ship anigh to wreck;
  Huge threatening waves swept wildly o'er the deck,
While helpless, hopeless, sick, the sufferers lay.

A timely tide — and He whose all times are —
  A woe inestimable averted then;
  Not yet a foremost one of earth's great men
Sank, as beneath the wave a glittering star.

THE fervid breath of Bengal's torrid sky
  Undid with haste the friendly sea-air's charm,
  And cooler climes must quell the quick alarm
That they had only fled from Death to die.

The youngest of the little flock was left
   Asleep in Earth's cold arms at Serampore,
   Where Christly eyes would watch his pillow o'er,
And Christly love would follow the bereft.

Let ours pursue them to the Isle of France,
   On a stanch ship whose name with JUDSON'S twines;
   The *Ramsey* — Captain HAMLIN,[59] in these lines,
A noble deed to score in happy circumstance.

This godly man his goodly ship would sail,
   For far Maulmain, Port Louis in her route;
   No Providence of Heaven would better suit
The Teacher's wish, and more his need avail.

The generous sailor generous offer made,
   And though in August blows the fierce monsoon,
   And they must toss beneath a windy moon,
Of India's sickness more than storms afraid,

The long, erratic voyage seemed the star
   Of hope, the pledge of healing to the sick;
   Their only wish beyond, — it might be quick,
That they could breathe the briny air afar.

Six weeks of storms, with brief lulls alternate,
   On Bengal's treacherous Bay the ship was tost;
   And with one dreadful crash they deemed her lost,
But God was with them in the awful strait.

Nor doubt we what His loyal servant wrote :
  "Two nights I have not closed mine eyes to sleep,
  But no weak terrors o'er my senses creep ;
In peace, to God my loved ones I devote."

Strength to the weak came on the storm-bird's wing,
  And genial breezes on the Isle of France
  Availed the wind's sweet healing to enhance,
Made pallid cheeks to flush, and white lips sing.

For six weeks yet across the Indian main,
  The *Ramsey* bore the grateful mission band,
  Their work pursued at sea as on the land,
And owned of God with saving grace again.

The noble ship their prayers a Bethel made,
  A house of God where He revealed His face ;
  And whispers, "Surely God is in this place,"
From rough lips fell, and contrite hearts betrayed.

The vessel through two moons at Maulmain lay,
  And ship and shore unwont communion kept ;
  And when she sailed, her crew and captain wept,
As mourned the elders on Paul's parting day.[60]

Not words alone, nor tears, revealed how much
  The sacred man had won the captain's heart ;
  His passage fees to Maulmain from the start —
As God's own gold — his hands forebore to touch.

THE Mission watchmen from their far-off tower,
    Prospecting Burma's wants, as years roll on,
    Saw one imperative need, — a lexicon, —
And for the task, a man with ample dower.

The Teacher, for the pulpit voiceless still,
    Was yet of marvellous gift of tongues possessed;
    And the great service, on his conscience pressed,
Constrained consent from his reluctant will.

The work assumed, he could not fail to bend
    His whole strong purpose to its doing well;
    That yet unfinished from his hands it fell
Finds reason in his sweet life's early end.

One half his plan he to its limit wrought;
    The English-Burmese[61] with consummate care
    And skill, if with his Bible we compare,
They seem alike with light and learning fraught.

A new home and new labor in Maulmain
    Were clouded yet with shadows of the grave;
    Domestic charms and sweetness could not save
The happy threshold from the feet of pain.

His dwelling rang with childhood's careless glee,
    And guileless sports his yet young heart beguiled;
    With the sweet Burmese prattle of each child
He taught them sweeter English on his knee.

But all the while the shadow deeper grew,
    And the fond mother's cheek beneath it paled;
    A third brief voyage down the coast-line failed
Her vigorous step and spirit to renew.


THE crisis called for change of clime, of life;
    No longer Burma's air, or Bengal's must she breathe;
    One only hope 'mid fears could love inwreathe
    Of snatching from the grave his noble wife.

Noble in all that makes a woman's worth,
    In gifts and graces both of heart and mind;
    In Burmese lore the Teacher scarce behind,
His helper lost, his affluence hence were dearth!

Of no mean skill in English prose and verse,
    Her facile pen was in translations free;
    Her gospel tracts and tender minstrelsy,
A myriad Burman tongues shall yet rehearse.

The Bible in the round Burmese she made
    Her study and devotion's daily bread;
    And could her life on heavenly air have fed,
Of tropic breath she had not been afraid.

Months on the wave, and happier months to spend
    Beneath her native skies and with her kin,
    By these alone the victory might she win
O'er maladies, else sure in death to end.

Nor must she in her weakness go alone
   Across the Indian and Atlantic seas,
   Bereft of loving care and ministries,
By ills beset, and by rude tempests blown.

Once and again had he the call denied,
   When worn with labors and with illness weak,
   Rest and new strength in his own land to seek,
Nor thought to leave his toils until he died.

If now the home-love in his heart o'ercame
   His sense severe of duty to his post,
   'T was not himself he loved, but her the most,
A sacrifice to duty still the same.

That he must leave the church without his care
   Racked deep with grief his sympathetic heart;
   Scarce more he felt the pain it was to part
With half his quiver full of children fair.

The elder of the flock 't were best should go
   For skilful nurture in their mother's land;
   Not yet to miss her loving, leading hand,
And into life's best grace and station grow.

Leaguered by hostile winds and wild, the ship
   Off the Mauritius sprung an ominous leak,
   That made it needful she repair should seek,
And at Port Louis let her anchor slip.

NOW marks my song a purpose great and brave,
   That here should sunder this heroic pair;
   She, so improved and less in need of care,
Should sail alone the wide Atlantic's wave.

He, with his Spartan courage, would return,
   Renew his battles with quaint Burman words,
   In the lone home-nest guard the little birds,
And let home's love-fire down to ashes burn.

Heroic will of his; brave her consent;
   Nor hers the less though steeped in love's hot tears,
   Which flowed in song of blended hopes and fears [62]
Of her sweet, sainted self our monument.

So nigh the purpose to its doing drew,
   The Teacher sent his Burman helpers back,
   Himself to follow by next ship their track,
And she her westward voyage to pursue.

Not thus the Arbiter of life and death
   Had on Time's dial set the hand for her;
   In swift relapse the danger signs recur,
And doubt hung darkly o'er her feeble breath.

Upon a ship our starry flag that bore,
   And soon would bear it to a native port,
   Of his tried soul the sea Hope's last resort,
They sailed together from the sea-isle's shore.

The Good Hope Cape with cool breath kissed the ship,
    And her faint smiles responded to the kiss;
    But ah! the flush was but a seeming bliss, —
A promise breathed, but fading at the lip.

At England's lone and famous sea-girt rock,
    Where her great foe so long her captive lay
    In life, — and death, till France removed his clay, —
Tolled her last hour supreme on Time's great clock.

While yet the ship at St. Helena stayed,
    Her last faint breath like dying infant's fell;
    And yet again we say, "Of Heaven 't was well"
Her blessed form was not in Ocean laid.

They dug her grave in Earth's strong bosom deep,
    Beside another saint's [68] — both far from home;
    Her tired feet had then no more to roam,
Her tender eyes naught more to do but sleep.

Oh martyred soldier of the Cross, who bore,
    That sacred eve, thy own great cross to sea,
    Our tears, our love, our praises follow thee —
As since to Heaven — to thy dear native shore.

HE stood a stranger on that native shore,
    Nor saw anear him one familiar face;
    Yet were there friendly arms for his embrace,
If none whose pressure he had felt before.

His wonderings where his little flock and he
   Should seek a fold to shelter them that night,
   And shrinkings else, were put to sudden flight,
By stress of eager hands and hearts in sympathy.

Happy the home where he might be the guest!
   A kinship broader than of blood and name
   Unnumbered bosoms stirred with love's warm flame
His path to honor through his native West.

What most he needed, still was least to find,
   Quiet and rest his shattered nerves to soothe;
   Not eager crowds and spreading palms could smooth
His path, still strewn with treasures left behind.

His feeble voice much public speech denied
   To throngs who flocked that charmèd voice to hear,
   Which rung through Burman zayats sweet and clear,
Yet for long years in his own tongue untried.

They saw his sad, sweet face, — and that to know
   As his, who thirty years his Master's cross
   Had borne with tears and toils and chains and loss
In pagan lands, — all else they might forego.

And yet not all. His own faint speech was sent
   In louder echoes of some voice well known,
   And by the press besides his words were sown
O'er the broad land, broadcast as where he went.

Through college halls and large assemblies ran
   Warm tides of mission influence, love, and zeal.
   What less than ardors could our churches feel,
To see and hear and know God's marvellous man?

By nature sensitive, reserved, and shy,
   He shrunk in pain from public eulogy;
   He saw not in himself what not to see
Left others dull of heart and dim of eye.

They saw, they felt, and could not help admire,
   With more than human pride and empty praise,
   How he had walked and toiled in hidden ways,
Who to earth's offered heights did not aspire.

Nay, but they knew earth had no nobler throne
   Than he had built his Master's cross beside,
   Yet knew not what he builded till he died,
And then by plaudit of his Lord alone.

How else than welcome him with love's applause
   And tributes wreathed with smiles and gemmed with tears,
   Could they whose hands and hearts for thirty years
With hopes and prayers and gifts maintained his cause?

Another generation lives since then;
   But through its life, from childhood to this hour,
   Its veins have throbbed with the seraphic power
Of mission zeal stirred by his voice and pen.

WHEN from June's hands her fragrant blossoms fell,
    And all his native land with verdure smiled,
    His heart from Burma could not be beguiled,
There only — this side Beulah — fain to dwell.

Words may not tell the anguish that he bore
    To give his children his last parting kiss.
    His sacred courage knew no rack like this;
It was for earth an absence evermore.

Only that here his daughter's life might take
    The grace and favor to her birthright due,
    And virtue's noblest ends his sons pursue,
He left them not for his but for their sake.

But his lone bosom, used to tender love,
    And the dear babes within the Burman nest, —
    With what new gift of God could both be blest,
Like wife and mother as their brooding dove?

He found her, and her heart was moved for him [64]
    From life's bright scenes and promise to depart;
    Already she had won his widowed heart,
And with devotion filled it to the brim,

In that her facile, graceful pen had wrought
    A picture fair and vivid to the life, —
    A sweet memorial of the angel-wife
He to her burial on the sea-rock brought.

If to his threescore years she gave her youth,
   The gift, if robbing her of fleeting fame,
   Repaid her with a new, immortal name;
And thus enriched her as did Boaz Ruth.

Her brightness blest his toils with vigor new;
   Her sweetness kept his changeful nature sweet;
   Her arm lent succor to his wounded feet;
Her truth made that of Heaven to him more true.

We bless her memory, hallowed now in death,
   For wifely love that cheered his latest years;
   Her life's brief mission in their light appears
Worthy of song like that of her own breath!

WHEN native ties were sundered for the last,
   And he for Burma sailed with his young bride,
   His heart and hope renewed at her brave side
The shattered strength of youth and manhood past.

He saw once more the lone rock in the sea,
   Where he had left his love in wakeless sleep;
   And blessed its friendly bosom, pierced to keep
Her precious dust till it should quickened be.

Five varied places of his dead he told,[65]
   Nor smiled his happy childhood's skies on one;
   The green earth had for him all service done,
His mortal form the sea-waves must enfold.

Once more to her who his new angel proved,
   He from the ship a burial-spot disclosed,
   Where 'neath the Hopia's friendly arms reposed
She first of him and half the world beloved.

From the twin narrow homes the young wife saw,
   Of those whose honored places she must fill,
   To liken them, what less than love's strong will
Could she, as Heaven's best inspiration, draw?

Although so sadly short the time for test,
   How nobly well her will to do was bent!
   With but four years of wifely duty spent,
This song may not declare her copy best.

Yet beautiful her self and service seem,
   Through ills that uncompared with prison-woes,
   Hunger and fright and sickness sore disclose,
That fill our vision like an ugly dream.

And one exceeding sorrow was her lot, —
   A depth of anguish to the twain unknown;
   They were not left of him on earth alone,
Widowed on heathen soil — where he was not.


ONCE more upon his chosen field of toil,
   He mingled tears and thanks before his God, —
   Tears for his little son beneath the sod,
And thanks the mission work had met no spoil.

At Maulmain, now beneath its English shield,
   The church in numbers and in graces grew;
   And laborers plenty, if fruits yet were few,
The mission cause his oversight might yield.

The burden on his soul was still to bear
   The freedom of the Cross to slaves of sin;
   From town and jungle trophies new to win,
And make the desert waste, with blossoms fair.

Such sacred toils his strength no more allowed,
   And one great duty on his hands was pressed;
   The new recruits were equal to the rest,
And to his language-work his will he bowed.

Fain had he gone to Ava, there to heed
   Haply some entrance to the nation's heart;
   And this denied, at least the royal mart
Would yield him books and scholars to his need.

For this no mandate and no means he gained;
   And to Rangoon he turned his troubled sight,
   Sad yet to go, from Maulmain's dawning light,
Where heathen darkness scarcely rifted reigned.

Yet learnèd men were there, and palm-leaves writ
   With Buddhist law and legendary lore,
   O'er which his scholar's quiet gaze might pore,
And for his ends gain some rare perquisite.

IN vain the bard has sought at old Rangoon
　　Some brightness on the young wife's path to
　　　　throw ;
　　His measures there would move alone to woe,
Save where her own sweet courage lifts the tune.

Her speech and laughter sweetened nauseous draughts,
　　And kindle smiles as we to tears incline —
　　To trace the well-masked ill in each light line
That to the eye her playful fancy wafts.

Their home, a haunt of noisome wingèd things, —
　　"Bat Castle" in her sportive dialect styled, —
　　Where she and hers were well-nigh going wild
From pests by day, and midnight whirr of wings.

Here while the tedious Buddhist Lent was kept —
　　For fifty years before less fast than feast ;
　　Its rigors now enforced by every priest,
Since royal eyes o'er rites no longer slept —

Nor flesh nor fowl might the pale strangers eat,
　　Of which a-sudden fell the food-stalls bare ;
　　And they were left, unwarned and unaware,
With fruit and sodden rice their only meat.

From meagre nurture and the fierce monsoon,
　　The castle now a hospital became ;
　　Hope in their hearts sunk to a feeble flame,
Forbid to stay, helpless to leave Rangoon.

No earthly succor for their wants appeared;
   Flight to Maulmain the season storms denied;
   And all their treasures there — O woe beside! —
The sudden doom of loss by fire had shared.[66]

NOW sunk the long-strained heart in unwont fear,
   And groans of torture from his lips escape, —
   " Haunted by foes, and ills of every shape,
Abroad forsaken, Death awaits us here!"

A moment's lapse, that folds a veil about
   His soul's strong faith, only that, lifting soon
   Like passing cloud across the lustrous moon,
'T will shine, from brief eclipse, the brighter out.

Again: " I count my sojourn here to be,
   Of life's whole desert, an oasis green,
   Since I have gathered from its darkest scene
Sweet fruits of faith in God's sufficiency."

And rarely fell a shade of dull despair
   On the serene of his love-lighted face;
   Heaven filled his soul with such transcendent grace,
That every feature caught some brightness there.

The " golden face " at Ava now was dark
   With direful menace to all foes of Buddh
   And Rangoon's fiendish viceroy eager stood,
In blood, to quench each native Christly spark.

But for the dread of Britain's arm so nigh,
    The Teacher's throat had felt the tyrant's hand;
    Fanatic fire had so inflamed the land,
That Christian proselytes and priests must die.

The monsoon's fierceness lulled, but not the wrath
    Of heathen hate to gospel men and words;
    These must be stilled by sharp and sudden swords,
Still daring trespass in forbidden path.

Defeat was sore to his undaunted breast,
    But every gain was loss in Death's fell front;
    Else had he braved it still, and borne the brunt
Of duty done, and left to God the rest.

TWO happy years of sweet domestic life
    And glad scholastic labors at Maulmain
    These sombre annals gild with joy again,
By dangers unassailed, in Rangoon rife.

Here to his humble home there flew a bird
    That nestled fondly on the mother's breast,
    And woke her rapture in such song expressed,
Its music round the listening world was heard.[67]

That daughter was not born with angel wings,
    And Heaven has spared her sweetness still to be,
    Of that dear nest, a living memory,
Till plumed for Eden, where her mother sings.

Here with his boys he was a boy again,
  In eager sport with them he led the play;
  Nor less he loved for those afar to pray,
His boys "at home," all linked in Love's bright chain.

Here with a glad — why not a proud? — delight,
  The last great labor of his life he closed;
  The English-Burmese Lexicon reposed,
In royal state, within his happy sight.

Here too he played the bishop of the fold,
  And lovingly he watched its welfare o'er.
  Sometimes he preached with fervor, as before,
And still the story of the Cross he told.

Sweet halcyon days, — a quiet breathing-spell
  And premonition of a longer rest,
  Yet so unwont to his laborious breast,
If sweeter than his toils he could not tell.


UPON this calm there fell a shade of ill;
  The brooding wing of widowhood he feared.
  The slow decline of her so much endeared
Might well his heart and home with anguish fill.

That brooding wing was spread, but not for her;
  Her young life rallied at the beck of love.
  The shadow lingered, though it seemed to move;
Another name was on Death's register.

Not long the "shining mark Death loves" he spared,
　　Now to the zenith of its brightness come;
　　Not rudely smote he all love's music dumb,
Yet with slow aim, but sure, his shaft prepared.

When months of wasting illness baffled skill,
　　And tender household ministries proved vain
　　To cool his fevered pulse and soothe his pain,
He found his solace in his Master's will.

Whom he for forty years had served in love,
　　He loved the more that he must serve the less;
　　Whom he had trusted through life's sorest stress,
Raised now his soul all fear of Death above.

Not yet the arrow flew to pierce his heart,
　　And to the healing sea-breath Hope yet clung;
　　Its play had ever made his spirit young,
And bade the weary, halting life-blood start.

A French ship, bound upon a voyage far,
　　At Maulmain[68] lay, impatient for the sea.
　　What else than happy omen could this be,
What less to Love's dark gloom than Hope's glad star?

Love through its blinding tears fond farewells said;
　　Borne to the ship by his disciples' arms,
　　Their tears the tokens of their love's alarms,
'T was love, still love, that his departure sped.

OUR short, impatient sense with chiding eyes
   Sees the good ship for weary days delayed
   Denied a warlike steamer's hoped-for aid,
While the pale sufferer pined for ocean skies.

So other partings, and one last from her
   Whom Love inspired, but Duty yet denied,
   To cleave in wifely fondness to his side,
While yet a breath his languid pulse should stir.

Death on the shore inevitable and near,
   And life — prolonged if not preserved — at sea,
   Words may not tell what deep, dumb agony
Distilled their final farewell to a tear!

Through five days on the blue and boundless main,
   Devout eyes saw that every rolling wave
   Was but his cradle rocking to the grave,
In whose soft depths should sink and cease his pain.

The waves rolled on, and swiftly sailed the ship;
   But when the sixth day's sun was in the west,
   The weary form was cradled for its rest,
And his great soul had let life's anchor slip.

His last words were of her, in two soft tongues, —
   His own by birth, and Burma's his in death, —
   "Care for poor mistress;"[69] and the loving breath,
With the sweet utterance, left the wasted lungs.

His life was great enough to fill with fame·
  The passing century, and its lines outlive;
  And still to Song and History halo give,
While speech shall catch the echo of his name.

In Nebo's bosom sleeps the sacred dust
  Of Moses, where — no burial-stone may tell;
  A broader grave befits our hero well,
The mighty deep his ashes holds in trust.

Men call thee treacherous, oh thou soundless sea,
  And many precious trusts hast thou betrayed;
  Deep in thy vaults a myriad dead are laid,
And Time, of few, the register will keep;

But ages wide shall not oblivion bring
  .Of his bright star that in thy waters set;
  And when thou art no more its glory yet
Beyond Time's Jordan shall its lustre fling.


MY song has lost its theme, since he is gone
    Whose life and love its lingering numbers filled;
    But ere what melody it makes is stilled —
  Look, friends, with me, his blessed shadow on.

He stands apart, single and separate,
  Amid the group of toilers in the field;
  Not to his claim, but to his right, we yield
The chiefdom of his broad Apostolate.

First on the soil of Burma he, to lift
   The blood-red banner of the Son of God;
   In faith (like that of Moses with his rod)
That he the flinty rock of Buddh should rift.

Himself so humble that, like Paul of old,
   He of the brethren held himself the least;
   Yet by his lowliness his height increased,
Till who to seek his stature is so bold?

He stands apart for what of God he wrought,
   And else for that his arduous toils are o'er;
   If one might rise to count his trophies more,
Yet single-armed he ne'er his battle fought.

Mark how he lived and labored, loved and lost;
   His life, loves, labors, losses, all were spent,
   From youth to age, with one supreme intent, —
To share with Christ the world's redemption cost.

Who shall his honors sum who may not look
   For records kept of toils and prayers and tears,
   Of tempests, trials, tortures, chains, and fears,
And their eternal outcome, in God's Book?

Beloved shade! That Book thine eyes have seen,
   And what thy faith foreknew thou dost behold;
   Great Gautama's spell from Burma backward rolled;
And gospel light its thousand rifts between.

Her tall pagodas tinkle yet their bells,
   But the sweet air that rings them now is free
   To thrill and swell with Heaven's high Jubilee,
Salvation by the Cross of Christ that tells.

THOU dost not marvel, that in old Rangoon,
   · Where o'er thee hung the headsman's bloody
       sword,
     If but thy lips proclaimed God's Holy Word, —
His servants preach and scatter it at noon.

Perhaps thou seest far beyond our sight,
   Which only yearns as yet for visions far ;
   Shining for thee not Burma's morning star,
But of its noontide sun the perfect light.

We may not know what glories meet thy gaze,
   Our eyes half blinded with the things we see ;
   While God has opened wide — it well may be —
For thy clear view, the scenes of future days.

Burma redeemed ! The Buddh by Christ replaced ;
   His proud pagodas ruined and o'erthrown ;
   His sun-clad priests to History only known,
And the crude Scripts on Palm-leaves all effaced.

If this thou seest there, oh shade divine !
   Thy steadfast faith has met its full reward ;
   Thou hast attained the knowledge of thy Lord,
As long, we know, His favor has been thine.

And do I dream that on thy heavenly face,
   I seem to see a sweet, seraphic smile,
   As thou from Heaven beholdest there the while,
No more at night, nor yet in secret place —

But in the day, and Gautama's dark frown —
   The sacred rite of Christ in Jordan done,
   For happy groups as thou at first for one,
Didst dare the cross, not seeing then the crown?

Beloved soul, translated to the skies,
   Our faith alone, as yet, can see thee there;
   But when, like thee, our fadeless forms we wear,
To Christ, the Lamb, our raptured songs shall rise!

# NOTES.

### Note 1, p. 1.

"*I sing of* JUDSON — *from his ardent youth,
With a strong zeal for Christian service fired.*"

ADONIRAM JUDSON was born at Malden, a picturesque suburb of Boston, on the 9th of August, 1788; and as the eldest son he received his father's name. The vignette on the titlepage of this volume is a picture of his birthplace as it appears to-day. His father was a Congregational minister, who nearly five years after the birth of this son removed to Wenham, and subsequently, in altered ministerial relations, to Braintree and Plymouth, among which several places the childhood and youth of young JUDSON were divided. Precocious and eager for knowledge, his father expected great things of his manhood, and by this expectation excited a strong ambition in the boy's mind. At the age of sixteen he was admitted to Providence College (now Brown University), and at the age of nineteen was graduated as valedictorian of his class. A successful teacher at the age of twenty-one, he prepared and published two acceptable text-books. Up to this period, 1808, his experience and life did not justify the text quoted as the basis of this note. His Christian zeal was not yet aflame;

and when it was kindled, it had, in spite of the thoroughly devout atmosphere he had breathed at home, and early religious impressions, to burn the rubbish of the sceptical philosophy which he had gathered during his college life. On closing his school in Plymouth, this happy change and its beneficent result were brought about by an incident which marked a tour he was making in the Northern States. At a hotel he slept in a room adjoining that in which was lodged a young man; and the landlord apologized for the necessity of placing him contiguous to one who was sick and nigh unto death. He made no protest against this, but inwardly queried what would be his own feelings if he were about to die; and he wondered if the invalid was a Christian, or, like himself, a sceptic. He heard in the morning that the youth was dead, and on inquiring for his name, was completely stunned by discovering that he was an intimate friend and classmate. Cutting short his tour, he went home an earnest inquirer for the way of salvation. This he found at the Seminary in Andover, and made a profession of his faith early in 1809, in his twenty-first year. From this date the couplet of our text acquires its justification. He was now zealous for his new Master; and the reading of Dr. Claudius Buchanan's famous sermon, "The Star in the East," was the occasion of kindling in his soul the flame which consecrated his youth and manhood and age alike to the cause of heathen evangelization. It may not be amiss to illustrate here the next stanza of the text following the couplet. He had, indeed, fair visions and bright prospects opened before him. Already he had been invited to the pastoral colleague-ship of the largest church in Boston, and he had declined a tutorship at his Alma Mater. His mind was made up to go to foreign lands as a missionary of the Cross of Christ.

There was then no Foreign Missionary organization in this country; and he, and others like minded with him, besought the General Congregational Union of Massachusetts to devise a plan for sending them among the heathen. This appeal brought into existence the American Board of Commissioners for Foreign Missions; the first, as even now it is in the extent of its work and means the foremost, of American Foreign Mission Societies, with a record for which every Christian heart is profoundly grateful to God. This Board sent the young candidate to England, to seek the co-operation of the London Missionary Society. His voyage was interrupted by the capture of the ship by a French privateer. He was imprisoned in France, and did not reach London until four months after he left Boston. His reception there was cordial, but it was not deemed advisable for the two Societies to act conjointly; and he returned home, to be sent speedily as an American missionary to Asia, or to whatever point seemed most promising of success in his work. As an important equipment for his work, he found a noble and lovely young woman willing to share his lot and his toils; and on the 5th of February, 1812, he married Ann Hasseltine of Bradford, Mass., then in her twenty-third, as was he in his twenty-fourth, year. On the 6th of that month he was ordained at Salem, and on the 19th he and his young wife set sail in the brig *Caravan* for Calcutta, beginning that "tortuous course" to which another note refers, and which had such marvellous issues as only the hand of God could have effected.

He died at sea on the 12th of April, 1850. Of the interval between his leaving Boston for Calcutta and his death, — an interval of over thirty-eight years, — his only vacation in the land of his birth was limited to nine months. The death of Mrs. ANN H. JUDSON occurred on the 24th of October, 1826, — making the period of her missionary life less than fourteen years — but a period so crowded with toils and trials, with sacrifices and sufferings, with patient endurances and heavenly devotions, as to constitute it a marvellous and scarcely paralleled era of womanly heroism.

From this point it is perhaps beyond the province of this note to extend biographical details.

## NOTE 2, p. 2.

*"On her lone grave, beneath the Hopia-tree."*

The Hopia-tree is considered the most valuable indigenous timber-tree in the southern provinces of India. It is often sawn up for building purposes, and is used extensively for boat-building. It is a flowering tree, and a prevalent variety of it is known as *hopia odorata*. Whether this is the variety that overshadows the graves of Mrs. JUDSON and dear little "Maria," or not, the writer has failed to learn. That special tree blooms, to the imagination and heart of thousands, with flowers suggestive of blossoms of Paradise. The charm of poetical description has been thrown around it, and it may be a welcome service that this note shall render to the reader, to reprint here the poem of Mrs. Sigourney written at the request of a dear friend, who sent her a branch from the tree, with a request that she would commemorate it in verse. We append the verses as they originally appeared.

### THE HOPIA-TREE.

Rest! Rest! The Hopia-tree is green,
And proudly waves its leafy screen
    Thy lowly bed above;
And by thy side, no more to weep,
Thine infant shares the gentle sleep, —
    Thy youngest bud of love.

How oft the feebly wailing cry,
Detained unsealed thy watchful eye,
    And pained that parting hour
When pallid Death, with stealthy tread,
Descried thee on thy fever-bed,
    And proved his fatal power!

"Ah, do I see, with faded charm,
Thy head reclining on thine arm,
    The 'Teacher' far away!
But now, thy mission-labors o'er,
Rest, weary clay, to wake no more,
    Till the great rising-day."


Thus spake the traveller as he stayed
His step within the sacred shade;
    A man of God was he,
Who his Redeemer's glory sought,
And paused to woo the holy thought
    Beneath that Hopia-tree.


The Salwen's tide went rushing by,
And Burma's cloudless moon was high,
    With many a solemn star;
And while he mused, methought there stole
An angel's whisper o'er his soul,
    From that pure clime afar,


Where swells no more the heathen sigh,
Nor 'neath the idol's stony eye
    Dark sacrifice is done;
And where no more, by prayers and tears,
And toils of agonizing years,
    The martyr's crown is won.


Then visions of the faith that blest
The dying saint's rejoicing breast,
    And set the pagan free,
Came thronging on, serenely bright,
And cheered the traveller's heart that night,
    Beneath the Hopia-tree.

## NOTE 3, p. 4.

*"Some names, as* XAVIER'S, *three dull centuries back."*

ST. FRANCIS XAVIER was a Spanish missionary, surnamed the *Apostle of the Indies,* and a disciple of Ignatius Loyola. His efforts were indefatigable and sincere, but as a modern writer expresses it, "They had not come to much; his successors had converted the heathen by becoming heathens themselves." Xavier was born April 7, 1506, in the Pyrenees, and died on Dec. 2, 1552, after ten years of various missionary toils.

## NOTE 4, p. 4.

*"And that of* SCHWARTZ, *far down the lonely track."*

CHRISTIAN FREDERICK SCHWARTZ was born at Sonnenburg, Prussia, Oct. 26, 1726, and educated at Halle. He went as a missionary to India in 1750, and settled at Tranquebar, on the Coromandel Coast. After fifteen years of labor in a Danish mission, he transferred his services to the English Society for the Diffusion of Christian Knowledge. He died at Tanjore, 1798. He was peculiar in his dress and habits, — wearing a black dimity robe, and living very frugally on $250 a year. He is said to have been of winning manners and of intense and holy devotion, "as courageous as John the Baptist, and his own life a pattern of what he called men to." When he died he was greatly lamented, Contemporary with him, and working in Bengal, was a Swede. named Zachariah Kiernander, who went in 1758 to Calcutta, at the invitation of Lord Clive, where he did some missionary labor, but with small result.

## NOTE 5, p. 4.

### "*When* CAREY *sailed from Albion's cliffs away.*"

WILLIAM CAREY, the founder and pioneer of Baptist Missions in India, was born in the village of Paulerspury, Northamptonshire, England, on the 17th of August, 1761. His childhood was passed in humble conditions of life, little removed from poverty,— his father being a weaver, although he was promoted to the two offices of parish clerk and schoolmaster. The boy was eager and enterprising; and while in after life he spoke of himself as "a plodder," he plodded so well that he laid the foundations, and eventually built the structure, of a great and memorable character.

Brought up in the Established Church, in early manhood he became a dissenter, in 1783 was baptized by one of the Ryland brothers, and his name is found in the list of members of a small church at Hackleton. In 1786 he became a settled pastor at Moulton, where he relinquished his occupation as a shoemaker (or "cobbler," as Sydney Smith designated him). His income as a preacher was, however, inadequate for even frugal living, and he resumed his trade, but in connection with his ministry. It was at Moulton that he conceived the idea of foreign evangelization; and so deeply was he impressed with the duty of this work, that he began at once to prepare himself and others for the then extraordinary enterprise of sending the gospel into heathen lands.

Always studious of books when he could obtain them, and not less of Nature, he acquired knowledge rapidly, and had a notable faculty for using it to the best possible advantage. Andrew Fuller relates that on entering his shop on one occasion, he found a large map pasted on the wall, made up of various sheets of paper, upon which were represented all known countries and notes of all he had read relative to their condition.

In 1789, at the age of twenty-eight, he removed to Leicester, maintaining his pastoral and mechanical labors diligently. Here he secured the friendship of Dr. Arnold, and revelled in his fine library. Here also he gave attention to science, and laid the foundations of his future botanical fame, which colored his after life in Serampore. The missionary idea was always in his mind and in his heart; and with the co-operation of such men as Andrew Fuller, Samuel Pearce, and the younger Ryland, he accomplished the formation of a Missionary Society at Kettering, in 1792. To a subscription which was taken up, and which amounted to about thirteen pounds, he contributed *himself*, although he did not, as was sensationally reported, do this by "*stepping into the collection plate.*"

The new Society did not at the outset make a deep impression upon the Baptist churches of England. The great city especially disregarded it, for its lowly birth-place. Nevertheless the hand of God was upon it, and the work, though hindered, and apparently baffled, by obstacles, went on; and in 1793 "CAREY *sailed from Albion's cliffs away.*" He took his reluctant wife with him, and his young son Felix (who was at Rangoon when the JUDSONS arrived there). They reached Calcutta, and the great East India Company considered their expedition too insignificant for hostile notice. The knowledge of the Bengali language was the first thing to be attained; and Ram Ram Bosu was secured as teacher, under whose tuition CAREY made rapid progress. As a supposed help to his success in his mission work, he undertook the superintendence of an indigo factory at Mudnabatty; and expecting it to be self-supporting, he wrote to the English Missionary Society that while he would do their mission work he would require no pay from them.

In 1796, the indigo works having proved unprofitable, he proposed the organization of a missionary settlement on the Moravian community plan, and offered to "throw his income and utensils into the common stock." This scheme was providentially delayed and defeated. In 1799 the indigo works were given up, and almost coincidently Messrs. MARSHMAN and WARD, and others, with their wives, reinforced the Mission; and soon thereafter, the East India Company developing hostility to their settlement in their territory, on the 10th of January, 1800, CAREY joined the Danish Mission settlement at Serampore, a sort of "city of refuge" for all disquieted people. It was a pleasant and healthful place, and it became "a little sanctuary for the Mission, and a centre of spiritual light and influence for the regions round about." Here it was that CAREY'S grand work took form and force. The Bible was now nearly all translated into Bengali, and the printing of it began. Boarding-schools were opened, and such effective means put into operation, that on the 28th December, 1800, Krishnu Pal, a native Hindoo, was baptized in the Ganges, together with Felix Carey, while other natives were "almost persuaded" to follow their example. Early in 1801 the New Testament was printed in the Bengali, and CAREY laid it reverently on the communion table of the Serampore church.

For thirty-four years after the settlement at Serampore, Dr. CAREY pursued his great work with unfaltering devotion and zeal. In 1829 suttee was abolished, and the proclamation declaring it to be criminal and punishable as homicide was sent to Dr. CAREY to be translated into Bengali. The order reached him on Sunday, as he was preparing for divine service. Throwing off his quaint black coat, he exclaimed, "No church for me to-day. If I delay an hour to translate and publish this, many a widow's life may be sacrificed." Resigning his pulpit to another, he summoned his pundit, and completed the translation by sunset. He had pleaded and prayed for the event ever since he reached India, and now for the first time during twenty centuries —

"The Ganges flowed unblooded to the sea."

Many years before the abolition of suttee and child-drowning in the Ganges, CAREY had sought this result, and hoped indeed, very early, to effect it through Lord Wellesley.

Great troubles and depressing disasters befell the Mission toward the close of Dr. CAREY's life, but the brave-hearted and noble old man never lost his faith in God, and never abated his zeal for the salvation of the heathen about him. "The last chord," says his biographer, "that vibrated in his heart was gratitude to God and His people for the favor shown to India. The eternal gates were opened for him at sunrise, June 9, 1834. . . . He was buried early next morning in the Mission burying-ground, where the dust of nearly three generations of native converts now reposes."

A contemporary wrote thus of this childlike saint: —

> "Thou 'rt in our heart with tresses thin and gray,
> And eye that knew the book of life so well,
> And brow serene as thou wert wont to stray
> Amidst thy flowers, like Adam ere he fell."

### NOTE 6, p. 4.

*"And suttee altar-fires no longer burn."*

The horrid funeral rite of suttee practised so long in India was abolished by the British Government in the year 1829, by the order of Lord WILLIAM BENTINCK, then Governor. If not ordained by Brahmin law, still it was sanctioned by it; and determined opposition to the act of the Government was made by Bengal Brahmins, while the people of India rejoiced greatly in its enforcement. It is said that after the British power was firmly established in India in 1756, and until Lord Bentinck's decree in 1829, not fewer than seventy thousand widows had fallen victims to this awful immolation.

### NOTE 7, p. 5.

*"Since Sydney thus the noble CAREY spurned."*

The disesteem in which foreign missionary efforts were regarded in their origin in England is well exemplified and emphasized by the bitter attack made upon them by the famous witty parson, Rev. Sydney Smith, in an article in the *Edinburgh Review* in 1808, from which the text is quoted. In 1809 he renewed his hostility, and took credit to himself for "routing out a nest of consecrated cobblers," with evident reference to WILLIAM CAREY, whom, however, he had not succeeded in "routing out." His language in this article is likely to be long remembered: "Our charge is that they want sense, conduct, and sound religion; and that if they are not watched, the throat of every European in India will be cut."

### NOTE 8, p. 5.

"*Though* SOUTHEY *taught — as, humbler, he had learned.*"

The attack of Sydney Smith originated discussion, and in 1809 it was closed by an elaborate article in the *Quarterly Review*, in which Southey glances over the history of missions to India, and particularly of those of the Baptist Missionary Society; and nearly at the close of the paper he says: "These low-born and low-bred mechanics have translated the whole Bible into Bengali, and by this time have printed it. They are printing the New Testament in the Sanskrit, the Orissa, Mahratta, Hindostan, and Gazarat; and translating it into Persic, Talinga, Karnata, Chinese, the language of the Sieks and of the Burmans; and in four of these languages they are going on with the Bible. Extraordinary as this is, it will appear more so when it is remembered that one of these men was originally a shoemaker, another a printer at Hull, and a third the master of a charity-school at Bristol."

### NOTE 9, p. 5.

"*From Kettering's altar England's churches caught,*" etc.

At Nottingham, in 1792, CAREY preached the Association Sermon, and thereby originated the Baptist Missionary Association.

The power of the discourse (from the text in Isaiah liv. 2, 3) was such that at the close of the assembly a resolution was passed to have presented at the next ministers' meeting at Kettering, "a plan for the establishment of a society for propagating the gospel among the heathen." At Kettering, Oct. 2, 1794, twelve men solemnly pledged themselves to God and to each other for such endeavor. Of these men were William Carey, John Ryland, and Andrew Fuller.

### NOTE 10, p. 6.

"*On the rude billows of the ocean tossed,*
*His long default tossed more his serious mind.*"

If the joint determination of Dr. and Mrs. JUDSON to connect themselves with the Baptist church at Calcutta was not actually reached by them during the voyages which preceded their arrival in India, there can be no question that the mental conflict from which that decision resulted took place on the restless bosom of the sea. There, too, the young pair, brought up in the fellowship of a noble Evangelical church and fondly attached to its communion, spent much time in discussion as to their duty, Mrs. JUDSON earnestly contending for the correctness of her life-loved views, even when her husband declared *his* conviction that they were erroneous. His son's testimony on this point is emphatic. There was indeed much to oppose such a conclusion, more than others can truly estimate. The sacrifice they must make was great and many-sided, and enough to appall their inexperience and their lonely position. Whether Mrs. JUDSON was decided *at sea* to take the solemn step of separation with him, or not, they had no sooner met the English Baptists at Calcutta than they mutually asked for baptism, and received the sacred rite at the hands of Rev. Mr. Ward, in the Baptist chapel at Calcutta, Sept. 6, 1812.

### Note 11, p. 7.

"*The sponsors lost he leaned upon before.*"

The young missionaries had been sent out by the American Board of Commissioners for Foreign Missions, and were dependent upon that great Society for their support and sympathy. The first of these essential succors they could not hope or desire to retain; and the consciousness that they might also lose the latter by the strangeness and suddenness of their action, and indeed must forfeit it at least for the time, wrung their hearts as perhaps no other conviction possibly could. They were without sponsors, for they had voluntarily given them up. To human sense their condition was a forlorn one, and they were human enough to feel this to their hearts' core. It is not to be wondered at that the American Board and the large body of Christians it represented took the surprising occurrence to heart, and regarded it at first wholly on the human side. Reproaches and condemnation were visited upon the poor friendless pair, who had thus "deserted their flag and their friends." It was indeed an anomalous and alarming crisis for them, but they knew, in the closest access of their pain and grief, that they had not deserted their best Friend; and this the sequel most strikingly, yea, marvellously, demonstrated. God had great designs to carry out through this wilful defection of theirs, as it was in itself, and for a time was so regarded and censured by those whom it offended and aggrieved.

### Note 12, p. 7.

"*And gathered there a broad and zealous band.*"

The almost immediate organization of an American Baptist Missionary Society followed the reception of the startling tidings of the baptism of Mr. and Mrs. Judson at Calcutta. It was interpreted by the American churches as a direct call upon them from the Great Head of the Church to engage earnestly in the work of sending the gospel to the heathen, and of taking the devoted missionaries now on the field, and mutely appealing to them for fostering care and loving sympathy, under their wing. This was done with glowing enthusiasm, and the great American Baptist Missionary Union of to-day is the outgrowth of that first Baptist Missionary Society formed on this continent. Into its hands exclusively Burma has fallen for the duty of its evangelization ; and a wonderful degree of prosperity has crowned the work, with continually increasing fruits in the multiplication of stations, the extensive formation of churches, the employment of native missionaries, and the establishment of Christian schools, colleges, and theological seminaries within the shadow of lofty pagodas and gilded zayats.

### NOTE 13, p. 8.

*" Nor soft resentment in their bosoms dwelt."*

Unwelcome as the tidings of Mr. and Mrs. JUDSON's change of denominational views, and of their union with the Baptist church at Calcutta, undoubtedly was at first to the great Society which had sent them out under its auspices, and equally to all the members of the Congregational churches, — to whom it appeared almost a dereliction of duty, — the feeling thus excited gradually softened; and as the evident leading of Divine Providence in the change became apparent, thanksgiving to God for the augmentation of force and zeal on the heathen field, and of Christian enthusiasm at home, took the place of resentment and even of regret, until to-day he whose defection grieved and offended them is honored and beloved and extolled, as no other servant of God in the broad annals of modern missionary service has ever been. At the departure, in September, 1888, from Boston, of a group of missionaries, — some returning to the Burman field and others going out for the first time — farewell services were held; and on the interesting occasion the Rev. Dr. Thompson, of the American Board of Commissioners for Foreign Missions, made a touching and eloquent address of congratulation, in which he declared the universal love and honor, extended by all connected with that great body, for JUDSON and his successors in Burma. This is doubtless true of all evangelical denominations throughout all lands. The courageous sacrifice of the JUDSONS has truly been owned and honored of God.

### NOTE 14, p. 8.

*" That famous guild of commerce and of might,*
*Which ruled the Eastern Indies by its arm."*

The hostility of the East India Company, which in that early period of British conquest and dominion in India really represented the Government, was due probably to the apprehension, largely felt, that the efforts of Christian missionaries to break up caste, and to replace the idolatrous rites of Brahminism and Buddhism with those of the Christian religion, would so inflame the hatred of the native princes and priests, that the new authority would be greatly imperilled and doubtless obstructed, if not overthrown. This apprehension, if ever of great force, was speedily overcome and banished by the interposition of Providential events; and for sixty years past the British flag has afforded its protection to missionaries wherever it has waved, and its prestige was their help throughout imperial Burma.

### NOTE 15, p. 9.

*" Seen in his tortuous course to that dark land."*

Receiving from the American Board of Commissioners for Foreign Missions an appointment as their missionary to the East, Mr. JUDSON sailed, with Mrs. JUDSON and Mrs. Harriet Newell, from Salem, Mass., for Calcutta. The voyage occupied four months. They were warmly welcomed by Dr. Carey, who was stationed at Serampore, only a few miles distant. Five months later he and his wife fled from expected arrest by the East India Company, which had ordered him to sail for England, and took passage privately for the Isle of France, having been refused permission to make the voyage. While sailing down the Hoogly River they were overtaken by a Government vessel, and forbidden to proceed. Soon, however, they were provided, without knowing by whom, with a passport to their desired haven, and were fortunate enough to overtake the ship from which they had been landed.

At St. Louis they heard of the death of Mrs. Harriet Newell, who sailed with them from Salem, and had just been buried on the Isle of France. Here they spent four months laboring among the English sailors of the garrison, not less eager, however, to pursue their voyage to the coast of India. They sailed then for Madras, hoping to establish a mission-post on Prince of Wales Island. At Madras they came again under the control of the East India Company, and finding there no ship to sail for the Island, and fearing immediate exile to England, they determined to sail — though in a crazy old vessel — for the port of Rangoon, in Burma, though dreading to pass from the protection of the English flag into the power of a heathen despot. They had a stormy passage to the Burman sea-port, and Mrs. JUDSON was so ill on their arrival there that she had to be carried on shore. This tortuous course occupied altogether seventeen months. At Rangoon they joined the Mission conducted by Felix Carey, the son of Dr. Carey of Serampore.

NOTE 16, p. 10.

"*Their sad, sole fruitage, — endless sleep at last.*"

This note might perhaps be more fitly placed in connection with the phrase, "Nigban's shadowy realm," in the next stanza but one, for they are broadly synonymous. "Nigban," or "Nirvana," is the end, the consummation, the crown, to which the purest Buddhist aspires; and it is attained, if at all, only after innumerable transmigrations and transformations of the votary. When attained, it is perhaps well defined by the expression, "endless sleep." It is certainly, despite of all glosses of interpretation and definition, a state of cessation from conscious being; and the phrase which Dr. JUDSON employed as its synonyme — " a blowing out" — seems to us, after a careful review of many vague and often contradictory opinions by the commentators on Buddhism, and especially on this condition, its supreme attainment, to be the best, as it is the briefest. Much objection is made by learned writers, and especially by writers more or less in sympathy with what they deem the grandeur of Buddha's philosophy, against the absolute and awful negation of immortality which "Nirvana" is charged with involving; but the historic record of the death of "Siddartha" makes him declare the *non-entity* of past, present, and future. The fearful succession of horrors which a Buddhist votary must pass through for almost interminable ages of time to reach Nigban at last may perhaps prepare him to welcome the barely possible realization of final extinction, — of being "blown out" as an expired candle.

NOTE 17, p. 10.

"*In vain the Palm-leaves noble doctrines teach.*"

We are indebted to Rev. W. F. THOMAS, of the Sandoway Mission, for the following concise and yet comprehensive note on the term employed in the text, to explain its significance in connection with Buddhist creeds. It is more musical in the verse than the term "Bee-di-gat." He furnished it to us just as he was about to return to his field of sacred toil: —

"The sacred writings of the Buddhist religion are usually scratched on strips of palm-leaf. These are fastened together between board covers, which are often highly ornamented. A number of these crude volumes are generally packed together in a basket, three of which are required to contain a complete summary of the Buddhist cult. Hence may have arisen the name *Pitika* (*Bee-di-gat* in Burma), or *Tri-pitika*, meaning 'baskets,' or 'three baskets,' applied to the three divisions embracing the whole range of Buddhist literature."

### NOTE 18, p. 11.

*"Siddartha's pictured grace, on Arnold's page."*

The founder of Buddhism is called Gautama, Siddartha, or Buddh. The first of these is the name of the family from which he sprung; Siddartha, his own individual name; and Buddha, "the enlightened one," the surname he acquired by his wisdom. It is believed that he was born about five centuries B. C., at Kapilvasta, near the foothills of the Himalayas, and a few days' journey from Benares. His father was an Indian prince, of the tribe of Sakyas, and Siddartha was brought up in the lap of luxury. Of a gentle and pensive disposition, he was carefully kept from any knowledge of human misery until he discovered it of himself; and learning that sorrow and death are the common destiny of all men, he then resolves to go forth as a homeless wanderer to seek out the way of deliverance from this doom for himself and his fellows. At first a Brahmin ascetic, he seeks pains and penalties; but relinquishing this quest, he meditates beneath the Bo-tree, and there discovers the way of salvation from the common doom. Then for half a century he travels far and wide, preaches his doctrines, and gathers a multitude of disciples; and at length returns to his home, where he lives to a great age, and dies breathing as his latest words, "There is nothing real, nothing durable." *This is the key-note of Buddhism.*

### Note 19, p. 11.

*"So, from the bright romance, our eyes decline  
To Paul's dark portrait of the heathen race."*

See Paul's Epistle to the Romans, i. 21–32.

### Note 20, p. 13.

*"And seeking him who taught it more to teach."*

The teacher employed by Dr. JUDSON as his instructor in the Burmese was a learned Buddhist, and had been a priest. Much discussion of a religious nature arose between them during study, and an interesting report of such a conversation is given in Dr. Wayland's "Memoirs of Dr. Judson," vol. i. pp. 171–174. This teacher was "a venerable-looking man in his sixtieth year."

### Note 21, p. 17.

*"A Christian zayat stands, complete and fair."*

A Buddhist zayat is especially, but not exclusively, a place for worship, and the name was adopted by JUDSON as appropriate to the uses of the Mission. In Rangoon, and other places, zayats were built as soon as it was deemed safe. Many heathen zayats are elegant if yet fanciful structures, and they are open at all times for heathen offerings to the idols. The first Christian zayat built in Burma was that referred to in the verse. It was destroyed in the Pegu-an War, but rebuilt.

### Note 22, p. 17.

"*When Burma's first disciple of the Cross.*"

This was a young man named *Moung Nau*. This prefix, *Moung*, expresses youth. That of *Ko*, advanced manhood. *Oo* is the title of an old man. The prefixes *Mee*, *Mah*, and *May*, indicate respectively a girl, a mature woman, and an old woman.

### Note 23, p. 22.

"*Vain hope! There beamed upon the "golden face."*"

The term "golden" was used to characterize all the features and belongings of the King and the Throne; and was also applied to the city where the Throne happened to be. Hence the expressions in the verse, "golden feet," "golden face," etc.

### Note 24, p. 26.

"*Known of twinned names which in high honor yield.*"

The arrival of the beloved recruits, Mr. and Mrs. WADE, was an occasion of inexpressible comfort and delight to Dr. JUDSON, and gave a new aspect and impulse to the great work. They reached Amherst Nov. 23, 1826, a month after the death of Mrs. JUDSON.

### Note 25, p. 26.

"*Great work the tireless Yüdathan had wrought.*"

The name "Yüdathan" was the nearest approach to the English pronunciation of the Teacher's name of which the Burmese tongue was capable, and it was sounded chiefly as if of three syllables, producing a musical and pleasing effect.

### Note 26, p. 27.

"*A home was ready there, as in a dream.*"

Of the building of this house, Mrs. JUDSON wrote thus: "We had but one alternative,—to remain in the boat till we could build a small house on the spot of ground which the King gave Mr. JUDSON. And you will hardly believe it possible—for I almost doubt my senses—that in just a fortnight from our arrival we moved into a house built in that time, and which is sufficiently large to make us comfortable."

### Note 27, p. 27.

"*Bandoola's troops flung forth the flag of war.*"

Bandoola was the only one of the Burmese generals who led his troops to victory in the war between England and Burma, which resulted at last so disastrously to the Avan King. He had gained slight successes in the British province of Arracan, and had sent at one time three hundred prisoners to the golden city as an evidence of victory. "The King began to think that none but Bandoola understood the art of fighting with foreigners. Consequently his majesty recalled him from Arracan with the design of his taking command of the army that had been sent to Rangoon. On his arrival at Ava, he was received at court in the most flattering manner, and was the recipient of every favor in the power of the King and Queen to bestow. He was, in fact, while at Ava the acting king." His expedition to Rangoon was an utter failure. He escaped to Dan-a-byoo with the loss of his army and ammunition, producing great consternation at court.

## Note 28, p. 28.

"*Meanwhile the 'golden city,' flushed with pride,
To its new palace welcomed back the King.*"

The "new palace" was built in the "golden city," which had alternated with Amarapoora (about six miles distant), as the royal capital. The old King had occupied the latter, but now a new and beautiful palace was built at Ava, and of this the royal household were to take possession, coming in state from Amarapoora for that purpose. The verses of the poem convey but a very inadequate idea of the splendor of the pageant which attended the taking possession of the costly structure.

## Note 29, p. 30.

"*The 'spotted face' of Death's stern servitor.*"

The executioner of the prison at Ava, called the "death prison," was, like all the "keepers," a branded criminal. These are called "children of the prison," and are a distinct and very degraded order, and excluded from all other classes. To see the "spotted face," or the "spotted man," was a vision dreaded as the premonition of death.

## Note 30, p. 31.

"*And thine, 'through deaths oft' (e'en as Paul's before).*"

See Paul's Second Epistle to the Corinthians, xi. 23.

## Note 31, p. 31.

"*That threatened peril to th' imperial state.*"

A year before the war the King had received from some foreigner the present of a noble lion, for which he entertained a very high regard, and caused him to be attended with special care. In the alarm that the war excited, and especially in view of the defeat and disgrace of Bandoola, it was whispered that, as the British bore a lion on their standard, it was probable that the noble beast which the King petted was a demoniac ally of the English troops. An ignorant, brutal fellow, the brother of the Queen, was the instigator of the rumors, and they produced their natural effect upon superstitious minds. The King made light of the whispers and strange glances that were heard and seen about the cage of the kingly beast. At length, however, he gave consent to the imprisonment in the death prison of the "suspect," but ordered that he should not be slain without his command. The Queen's brother gave secret directions that he should not be fed. The story of the slow and terrible process of starvation which resulted in the death of the tortured animal is related by Mrs. JUDSON in her account of the death prison, and is a very harrowing tale. When, at last, the raving and roaring of the poor beast ended, and the cage stood empty in the prison yard, Mrs. JUDSON succeeded in obtaining permission to make of it a room for her husband, which was sumptuous in comparison with his cell in the prison. This permission, refused by "*the cat*," as the head jailer was called, was granted by the "governor" of the prison.

NOTE 32, p. 32.

"*A cruel, traitorous pakan-woon had gained,*
*By subtlety and fraud, the Emperor's ear.*"

The *pakan-woon* and *lamine-woon* were officials, not of state but of communities, similar perhaps to the mayors of cities and towns among us, though invested with more power than these, and using it in a very arbitrary and often lawless manner. The *woon-gyee* was a state officer.

## Note 33, p. 32.

*" And tithed the ticals gathered for their pay."*

The tical is a Siamese coin, but has currency in Burma. Its value differs very little from that of the rupee, and may be reckoned, with allowance for its changing value, at an average half-dollar. It is described as a bean-shaped piece of silver. Small transactions in money are sometimes made by cutting sheets of lead and silver, or their alloys, into pieces, which go by their weight.

## Note 34, p. 32.

*" The scene is shifted now to Oung-pen-la."*

The little village, or hamlet, of Oung-pen-la is situated a few miles only from the "golden city," but was reached from the hot, sandy shore of the Irawaddy by a track of about four miles in a rude cart. It was destitute of any shops or any conveniences for the comfort of visitors, whether voluntary or constrained, and leaves upon the reader's mind the impression of desolateness. The name was itself a terror to prisoners sent from Ava.

## Note 35, p. 34.

*" To Amarapoora and its lamine-woon."*

The *lamine-woon*, like the *pakan-woon*, was a sort of municipal officer. It would seem that there were a few drops of the milk of human kindness in the bosom of the chief of Amarapoora, into whose hands the missionaries fell, for he permitted Mrs. Judson and her attendants to go to Oung-pen-la.

### NOTE 36, p. 36.

"*Till o'er the hamlet by transmission stole  
The hateful ill in sequence sure but mild.*"

The process of inoculation, as a mitigation of that terrible malady, the small-pox, was introduced into England a hundred and fifty years ago, and was not entirely superseded by vaccination in the first quarter of the present century. Its use was advocated as a certain alleviator of the attack of the malady, and the remarkable application of it by the heroic missionary wife at Oung-pen-la was the best resource she had, and fortunately proved exceedingly beneficial.

### NOTE 37, p. 37.

"*That dreadful march from Let-ma-yoon's felt gate.*"

Let-ma-yoon is the name of the otherwise-called "death prison" at Ava. Its meaning is very expressive, implying the hopeless character of the confinement within its walls. It signifies, by its succession of monosyllables (each of them being a distinct word, which is characteristic of the Burmese language), "*Hand, shrink not.*" Ava's place of death was indeed well named.

### NOTE 38, p. 40.

"*With fevered strength she gained her medicine-chest.*"

When Mrs. JUDSON followed her husband to Oung-pen-la, she left in the mission-house all her household goods, save only those which, retained from the first confiscation of her effects, were still in the keeping of the authorities. Among these was her invaluable medicine-chest; and the recovery of this on her enforced visit to her home in Ava occasioned her much anxiety and trouble, and probably she would not have secured it but for the kind feeling of the governor of the North-gate, who had before shown her much favor and a true sympathy.

### NOTE 39, p. 40.

*"But still the clumsy cart-wheel blocks must creep."*

Mrs. JUDSON refers to this terrible journey in her description of their life at Ava and Oung-pen-la, and says: —

"You may form some idea of a Burmese cart when I tell you that its wheels are not constructed like ours, but are simply round, thick planks with a hole in the middle, through which is thrust a pole that supports the body."

### NOTE 40, p. 41.

*"A faithful fellow he, guardian and cook."*

Of the service and fidelity of this Brahmin servant Mrs. JUDSON herself says, in a letter to her brother: "A common Bengalee cook will do nothing but the simple business of cooking; but he seemed to forget his caste, and almost his own wants, in his efforts to serve us. He would provide, cook, and carry your brother's food and then take care of me. I have frequently known him not to taste of food till near midnight, in consequence of having to go so far for food and water, and in order to have Mr. JUDSON'S dinner ready at the usual hour. He never complained, never asked for his wages, and never for a moment hesitated to go anywhere or to perform any act we required. I take great pleasure in speaking of the faithful conduct of this servant, who is still with us and, I trust, has been well rewarded for his services."

It is our delightful privilege to add to this testimony the grateful fact that after ten years of such devotion this noble fellow gave evidence of true conversion to Christianity, and was baptized by Dr. JUDSON.

### NOTE 41, p. 41.

*" Two months within that stifling chamber lay*
*The mother's form upon the paddy heap."*

The reader is already aware that the little room Mrs. JUDSON and her girls occupied in the jailer's house was half filled with rice in the husk, over which mats and wraps were spread for sleeping. This unhusked rice is the "paddy" of Burma.

### NOTE 42, p. 42.

*" That they to Buddh's first Hell by fire should go."*

The Buddhist religion recognizes eight principal hells, of which the first four are governed by heat, and the second four by cold. Besides these there are numerous lesser hells; sixteen, indeed, are said to surround each of the superior hells, — making in all an aggregate of one hundred and thirty-six of these places of torment. From some of these hells there is no deliverance, as in the case of great criminals. From others, and perhaps the greater number of them, deliverance may come after immense periods of endurance of indescribable tortures, through "merits" while under penalty. In such cases the victim may enter, on his deliverance, upon a new existence by transmigration, and may become an insect, a bird, a reptile; and, through successive transformations, may attain the character of a *nat*, which is a spirit. The periods of existence in successive transmigrations are of great length. The severest penalties are attached to disrespect of the priesthood and atrocious crimes generally. The "brazen hell," to which reference is made in the poem as the fate of the unhappy pakan-woon who defrauded his soldiers and lost in battle the stronghold of Pugan, is described as a vast caldron of molten brass, the descent of the victim to the bottom of which requires a period of three thousand years, and for the return ascent to the surface a similar fearful term of years. The descriptions given in Buddhist books of the experiences of victims in the various hells are too revolting to be minutely repeated. They are, however, distinctly and emphatically demonstrative of the Buddhist belief in prolonged existence and also in retribution.

### NOTE 43, p. 44.

"*No smile to greet him at Maloun's war-gate.*"

Maloun was the camping-place of the Burman forces on the Irawaddy. It was stormed by the British forces on the 19th of January, 1826, a month before the treaty of peace was signed at Yandabo.

### NOTE 44, p. 45.

"*Five million rupees — the redemption fee!*"

The rupee is a coin of varying value, according to its local coinage. The present commercial value in our exchanges is about forty cents, but it is safe to estimate it at fifty cents. The depreciation of silver has wrought a change in its market worth. The amount therefore demanded by the English commander from the Emperor of Ava, as the condition of safety to the "golden city," may be stated at nearly two and a half million dollars!

### NOTE 45, p. 47.

"*Came, with the envoys, slight encouragement,
In easier terms the hundred lacs to pay.*"

A *lac* of rupees is one hundred thousand, and at that time was equivalent to about forty-five thousand dollars.

## NOTE 46, p. 55.

*"Forged by Alampra's prowess and renown."*

Alampra, whose truer name was Aloung Pra, was the most celebrated warrior king in Burman history. About the middle of the eighteenth century, the Pegu-ans, who had been in subjection to the Kingdom of Ava for a long period, broke the yoke and resumed their independence. They did not, however, long maintain it, for Alampra gathered a large army, and made effective war upon the revolted province, which he brought, with a number of neighboring provinces, into his own dynasty. The attempt of the Pegu-ans, during the British War with Ava in 1824, to regain their independence was ineffectual, though it involved the Mission interest in Rangoon, while that port was invested by the enemy, in disaster. The Pegu-ans are the people now known as the Taligns, among whom the missionaries are laboring with great success.

## NOTE 47, p. 57.

*" Into the mission treasury hence he told*
*The generous gains his civic service won."*

The Board of Managers of the Missionary Union, acting upon suggestions made to them by Dr. JUDSON, in 1826, as to the fiscal relations of missionaries to the Society, adopted the same without modification. Dr. Wayland, in his Memoir, says:—

"In consequence of this decision, Dr. JUDSON made over to the Board five thousand two hundred rupees,—the sum allowed him by the Governor General in council, in consideration of his services at the treaty of Yandabo, and as a member of the embassy to Ava; and also two thousand rupees, the avails of presents made to him at Ava. This was frequently spoken of as a donation to the Mission. He, however, never so considered it. In conveying it to the Board he acted only in conformity with the principles he had adopted, and by which he believed every missionary should be governed. If he had retained it, no one could have found just cause of complaint; for during these months little could have been done for the Mission. He appreciated, however, the value of the principle, and refused to receive any higher remuneration than was received by his brethren, considering all the surplus the rightful property of the Mission."

NOTE 48, p. 59.

*" When one half more the sun had run his round."*

The scientific reader will doubtless smile at the introduction of a note aiming to disembarrass the mind of any one who may not at once perceive that this verse refers to the apparent motion of the sun through the signs of the Zodiac, which is only by a poet's license synonymous with the simpler expression, — *six months later*.

NOTE 49, p. 59.

*" The Teacher made Maulmain his fixed abode."*

Dr. JUDSON and the English Civil Commissioner, Mr. Crawfurd, had gone up the beautiful Salwen River to select a site for the new capital of the province ceded to England by the Yandabo treaty. The result of their expedition was the choice of a location on a promontory near the mouth of that river, where it pours its rushing waters into the sea. It was a beautiful and salubrious spot, and the missionaries hailed it with delight, in exchange for unhealthy and unlovely and unsafe Rangoon. This town was named Amherst, in honor of the Governor General of India. Here Mrs. JUDSON was buried, and here also the little girl who was nursed in the prison precincts of Oung-pen-la; and here they expected to abide in prosperous mission-work. But an unfortunate disagreement between the Civil Commissioner and the Commander-in-chief of the victorious army defeated this plan. General Campbell preferred altogether the site of Maulmain, then a small town but about twenty-five miles farther north than Amherst, and nigher the wide mouth of the Salwen. The Commander considered it a more strategical point than Amherst, and this decided the fate of the latter place. It was a hard thing for the Teacher to leave his graves under the Hopia; but at Maulmain the army was posted, and thither the people were flocking from Amherst, and also from the dominions of the tyrannic King of Ava. It was thus that Maulmain became the capital of Tenasserim, the great site of the American Baptist Mission in Burma, and the home of the beloved JUDSONS for more than a score of years.

### NOTE 50, p. 64.

#### "*An old disciple thus had shown his love.*"

It afterward transpired that this beautiful act had been done by an aged deacon of the Maulmain church, Ko Dwah, who was devotedly attached to the Teacher. Ko En communicated this fact to Mrs. SARAH B. JUDSON. Both Ko Dwah and the beloved Teacher were taken sick at nearly the same time; and when Dr. JUDSON was carried to the boat by the disciples, the aged man was not able to accompany them, so they met no more on earth after a single interview during their illness. When the old deacon learned that the Teacher had departed, and his house had been torn down as unhealthy, he hobbled out of his dwelling to see the ruin, and mounting the chapel steps with great pain, he bowed his face on his hands and uttered a wailing funereal cry. He did not long survive the shock to both mind and body.

## Note 51, p. 65.

"*He from the spell to brighter zeal awoke,
Forgot the open grave until he died.*"

"He had suffered much," says Dr. Wayland, in his Memoir, "from a peculiar form of dread of death, — not the separation of the soul from the body, or any doubt of ultimate acceptance with God; but a nervous shrinking from decay and corruption, the mildewing and mouldering in dark, damp, silent ghastliness. He believed this to be the result of pride and self-love, and in order to mortify and subdue it, he had a grave dug, and would sit by the verge of it, and look into it, imagining how each feature and limb would appear, days, months, and years after he had lain there."

## Note 52, p. 66.

"*There Ko-thah-byu the one Great Teacher found,
And to his countrymen the Christ made known.*"

There is, perhaps, in all the records of conversions in Burma, no single one of greater interest than that of the poor Karen bondman, Ko-thah-byu. He accepted the gospel when it was proclaimed to him, with eagerness and joy, and speedily communicated its glad tidings to some of his wild countrymen, bringing them, as he had opportunity, to the Christian teachers. When he had received baptism, in 1828, he became at once a missionary, and earned, by his devotion and zeal in seeking the conversion of his brethren, the title of the *Apostle of the Karens*. This people had at first no written language; and when their rude dialect was reduced to form and writing by the missionaries, they soon appreciated the benefit conferred upon them. From their traditions they were looking for sacred teachers, and were thus inclined to listen eagerly to Ko-thah-byu and to the white teachers. The beloved Boardman and his faithful wife welcomed many of them to Christ in their own rude villages, and also at Tavoy. As an illustration of the spread of the Gospel among these simple but sincere people, and also of the relation of Ko-thah-byu to the grand result, it may be stated here that in 1878 the jubilee of his baptism was celebrated in Tavoy by the dedication of a Memorial Hall built by Karen Christians at a cost of nearly thirty thousand rupees. It represented *more than as many Karens converted during the previous fifty years!*

### NOTE 53, p. 67.

"*Like twinkling stars before the ampler room,
The risen sun shall, at God's noon-time, bless.*"

The success of the mission-work among the wild mountain tribes of Burma, though remarkable during the life of JUDSON and his co-laborers, — especially the beloved Boardmans, — has been so signal of later years that it is almost as if " God's noontime" for that remarkable people was close at hand. The sun of righteousness is indeed pouring its splendid radiance into the valleys, over the wooded hills, and along the sparkling and flashing rivers, where these simple-hearted tribes are found. The statistics of the present time are exhilarating and assuring to the faith of every Christian soul. There are now nearly fifty missionaries, men and women; four hundred and sixty native preachers, one fifth of whom are ordained; about five hundred churches; and over twenty-six thousand members, of whom nearly two thousand were baptized during 1887. It is questionable if this gospel success is exceeded upon any mission-field in all India; and if equalled by the Telugu Mission, it is certainly not by any other.

## Note 54, p. 69.

"*As bricks, aforetime, without straw were made.*"

See Exodus, v. 7, 8. The stubble which the captives were compelled to gather for themselves was so poor a substitute for the straw denied them, that the negation of the verse is at least constructively justified.

## Note 55, p. 72.

"*Rich sunset glories gilded old Prome's pride,
Her god Shway-San-dau gleaming on their boat.*"

The magnificent pagoda *Shway-San-dau* was to Prome what the *Shway-Da-gong* is to Rangoon, and the *Kyaik Thanlan* to Maulmain. The picture of Shway-Da-gong accompanying this poem will serve for a type of all these pagodas, — splendid, if sometimes chiefly with gilding and tinsel. The prediction of the downfall of the great glittering Prome idol, so touchingly uttered by Dr. Judson, is already coming to pass, and the fading glories of Shway-San-dau will hardly be renewed.

## Note 56, p. 74.

"*Besides the Gospels and the 'Scrippet' leaves.*"

Dr. Judson was wont to speak half playfully and half impatiently of the abundant single pages issued from the Maulmain press, which he called "Scrippets," and was loath to give to inquirers in the stead of larger tracts and whole gospels, — too seldom, he felt, at his command for distribution.

## NOTE 57, p. 78.

"*Karens, Taligns, and Burmans to the Cross
From Buddhist idols and pagodas turn.*"

The Taligns, only here thus named in the poem, are the Pegu-ans, who have a dialect of their own, which has been in business affairs superseded by the Burman, and is therefore now of little account. They are, however, a numerous people, and have become of great interest to the missionaries, whose recent successes among them are very remarkable and encouraging.

## NOTE 58, p. 80.

"*He let occasion slip, and felt the loss.*"

He himself realized that he had made a mistake in limiting his previous voyages to short excursions along the coast, or even to Bengal; since he assured himself, and was indeed advised, that the air of the open sea, breathed for weeks, would probably work a beneficial result in his case.

## NOTE 59, p. 81.

"*The* Ramsey — *Captain* HAMLIN, *in these lines.*"

The piety and generosity of this noble man, as exemplified in the voyage to which the text refers, demand this note. His ship was really a Bethel, and some of the officers and sailors were hopefully converted. At the close of the long voyage he not only refused to receive the passage-money due him, but he returned four hundred rupees which Dr. JUDSON sent him after his refusal to make a charge which might justly have been three or four times that sum. His kindness was acknowledged by the Board in a resolution of thanks sent to him, with valuable religious books.

### Note 60, p. 82.

"*As mourned the elders on Paul's parting day.*"

The Apostle of the Gentiles, on one of his missionary tours, landed at Miletus; and, pressed for time, resolving to sail by Ephesus, he sent thither for the elders of the church there to meet him at Miletus. The narrative of their visit and the Apostle's touching address to them are detailed in the latter half of the twentieth chapter of The Acts. The concluding verses read thus:

"And when he had thus spoken, he kneeled down and prayed with them all.

"And they all wept sore, and fell on Paul's neck and kissed him;

"Sorrowing most of all for the words which he spake, that they should see his face no more."

### Note 61, p. 83.

"*The English-Burmese with consummate care.*"

The second part of the great Burmese Lexicon — the Burmese-English — which Dr. JUDSON began, and for which he prepared much material, he did not live to finish. A few days before his death he requested that his manuscripts relating to it should be transmitted to his friend and associate Mr. Stevens, by whose hands the noble work was carried to completion. It remains a monument of industry and learning not exceeded in mission annals.

### Note 62, p. 86.

"*Which flowed in song of blended hopes and fears,
Of her sweet, sainted self our monument.*"

The readers of this poem to whom the song here referred to is familiar would doubtless wonder if it were not included with the

"Notes;" and to those who have not met with it in their reading, it cannot fail to give a new pleasure. Its presentation, therefore, at this point needs no apology. It beautifully exemplifies the tender spirit and the fine poetic taste of the noble Christian woman from whose heart it sprung.

## A PARTING SONG.

We part on this green islet, Love, —
  Thou for the Eastern main,
I for the setting sun, Love, —
  Oh, when to meet again?

My heart is sad for thee, Love,
  For lone thy way will be;
And oft thy tears will fall, Love,
  For thy children and for me.

The music of thy daughter's voice
  Thou 'lt miss for many a year;
And the merry shout of thine elder boys
  Thou 'lt list in vain to hear.

When we knelt to see our Henry die,
  And heard his last faint moan,
Each wiped the tear from other's eye;
  Now, each must weep alone.

My tears fall fast for thee, Love;
  How can I say — farewell?
But go, — thy God be with thee, Love,
  Thy heart's deep grief to quell!

Yet my spirit clings to thine, Love,
  Thy soul remains with me;
And oft we 'll hold communion sweet,
  O 'er the dark and distant sea.

> And who can paint our mutual joy,
>   When, all our wanderings o'er,
> We both shall clasp our infants three,
>   At home, on Burma's shore?
>
> But higher shall our raptures glow
>   On yon celestial plain,
> When the loved and parted here below
>   Meet, ne'er to part again.
>
> Then gird thine armor on, Love,
>   Nor faint thou by the way,
> Till Buddh shall fall, and Burma's sons
>   Shall own Messiah's sway.

### NOTE 63, p. 87.

*"They dug her grave in Earth's strong bosom deep,
Beside another saint's — both far from home."*

The reference here is to Mrs. Chater, who was for a number of years a faithful and honored English missionary at Ceylon, and who died at St. Helena while on her homeward voyage for the restoration of her health. The funeral services at the burial of Mrs. JUDSON were impressive, and accompanied by such touching manifestations of Christian sympathy and generosity as deeply affected the heart of the bereaved and afflicted "Apostle of Burma," who was obliged to resume his voyage on the evening of the burial day.

### NOTE 64, p. 90.

*"He found her, and her heart was moved for him."*

The story of the third Mrs. JUDSON's life has been very graphically told by Professor A. C. KENDRICK, to which the interested reader is referred. Dr. JUDSON's meeting with her was at the house of a mutual friend; and when in conversation with her, the great 'missionary half chided her for the lightness of her literary productions as "Fanny Forrester," she so artlessly and effectually vindicated herself that the Doctor challenged her to try her pen on a memoir of the beloved wife he had buried at St. Helena. She consented, and to her interest in the task she undertook, she added an interest in the distinguished man who thus employed her. The sequel is known to our readers, and if at the time of their marriage the religious world and the social world murmured alike, the former at least is not only satisfied, but grateful to God for the Providence which brought them together, realizing, to her, a half-unwelcome presentiment that she should one day be a missionary to the heathen, and becoming to him a most admirable successor of two such wives as were ANN HASSELTINE and SARAH BOARDMAN. Her missionary memorials are touching and tender; and her service to the Apostle of Burma, during the four years for which they continued, are cherished in all Christian hearts. Her own death, four years later, was deeply lamented, It occurred at Hamilton, N. Y., June 1, 1854, eight years and one day after her romantic but heaven-hallowed marriage. Her daughter survives her, and is now the honored wife of the Rev. W. T. C. Hanna of Ballston, N. Y.

NOTE 65, p. 91.

"*Five varied places of his dead he told.*"

These were as follows: —
1. At Rangoon, his infant son ROGER WILLIAMS.
2. At Amherst, Mrs. ANN H. JUDSON and her dear little "MARIA," under the Hopia-tree.
3. At Serampore, his son HENRY.
4. At Maulmain, two children.
5. At St. Helena, Mrs. SARAH B. JUDSON.

### Note 66, p. 95.

"*The sudden doom of loss by fire had shared.*"

In the midst of their untoward and distressing experiences at Rangoon, they received intelligence of the burning of a house in Maulmain in which they had stored their best wardrobe and most valuable effects, including especially some important manuscripts and many cherished presents from lost friends. It was felt as a great calamity, but their Christian faith and trust in God enabled them to bear it with serene if yet sorrowful patience.

Dr. JUDSON, writing to another missionary, — Rev. E. A. Stevens, a sharer in the great loss, and at the time of the fire dwelling in the burned house, — says : "' The Lord gave, and the Lord hath taken away : *blessed be the name of the Lord.*' My heart overflows with gratitude, and my eyes with tears, as I write these precious inspired words. There are some other lines, quaint in garb but rich in core, that are worth more than all your house and contents : —

> ' Blessed be God for all,
>     For all things here below;
> For every loss and every cross
>     To my advantage grow.'

"But I sympathize with you and dear Sister Stevens. Brother Bullard has also sustained a heavy loss. Brother Brayton's will not, on the whole, be any great loss. As to me — the leeks and onions that were packed up in those two valuable boxes — worth about seven or eight hundred rupees — were very bright to the eye and soft to the feel ; and many of them we shall greatly need, if we live a year or two longer ; but they have gone to dust and ashes, where I have seen many bright, dear eyes go, to rescue any pair of which I would have given those boxes ten times over.".

## NOTE 67, p. 96.

*"Its music round the listening world was heard."*

It is safe to say that, dainty and delicate as were many of the poetical effusions of "Fanny Forrester," none of them surpassed, if indeed they equalled, the poem with which, as EMILY C. JUDSON, she greeted the birth of her babe at Maulmain, and which we cannot here withhold from the reader: —

### MY BIRD.

Ere last year's moon had left the sky
  A birdling sought my Indian nest,
And folded, oh, so lovingly!
  Her tiny wings upon my breast.

From morn till evening's purple tinge
  In winsome helplessness she lies;
Two rose-leaves, with a silken fringe,
  Shut softly on her starry eyes.

There's not in Ind a lovelier bird;
  Broad earth owns not a happier nest;
O God, Thou hast a fountain stirred,
  Whose waters never more shall rest!

This beautiful, mysterious thing,
  This seeming visitant from heaven, —
This bird with the immortal wing,
  To me, — to me, Thy hand hath given.

The pulse first caught its tiny stroke,
  The blood its crimson hue, from mine;
This life, which I have dared invoke,
  Henceforth is parallel with Thine.

> A silent awe is in my room;
>   I tremble with delicious fear;
> The future with its light and gloom —
>   Time and Eternity — are here.
>
> Doubts, hopes, in eager tumult rise;
>   Hear, O my God! one earnest prayer, —
> Room for my bird in Paradise,
>   And give her angel-plumage there!

### NOTE 68, p. 98.

*" At Maulmain lay, impatient for the sea."*

This note refers only to the name of the city where lay the French ship, *Aristide Marie*. It is probably known to the reader that the British Government has now established the spelling of that city's name as Moulmein, instead of Maulmain, as it appears all through the poem. We deemed it proper to preserve the old orthography, as not only familiar to all readers of the Burmese mission records and memoirs, but especially as that which alone was known to Dr. JUDSON. Our associations with it, for his sake, endear the old-time spelling.

### NOTE 69, p. 99.

*"' Care for poor mistress;' and the loving breath
With the sweet utterance left the wasted lungs."*

This tender injunction was addressed to his devoted and faithful servant, whose assiduous ministries, together with the sympathies of a brother missionary, served to soothe the anguish of his last hours. "His death," says Mr. Ranney, "was like falling asleep."

www.ingramcontent.com/pod-product-compliance
Lightning Source LLC
Chambersburg PA
CBHW030247170426
43202CB00009B/654